METAMORPHOSES

IN TWO VOLUMES

METAMORPHOSES OF THE SOUL

Paths Of Experience

RUDOLF STEINER

18 Public Lectures 1909-10

VOLUME ONE

9 Public lectures given between
14th October and 9th December 1909
in the Architect's House, Berlin

Translated by C. Davy and C. von Arnim

RUDOLF STEINER PRESS
LONDON

First published in English 1930
(translated by G. Metaxa)
Second Edition 1983

The German title containing these lectures is *Metamorphosen des Seelenlebens und Pfade der Seelenerlebnisse*, published in two volumes by the Rudolf Steiner Verlag, Dornach, Switzerland (Nos. GA58 and GA59 in the Bibliographical Survey, 1961). This English edition is published in agreement with the Rudolf Steiner Nachlassverwaltung, Dornach, Switzerland.

No part of this book should be reproduced in any form without prior permission from the copyright holder. All rights are reserved.

© 1983 Rudolf Steiner Press, London.

British Library Cataloguing in Publication Data

Steiner, Rudolf
   Metamorphoses of the soul.—2nd ed.
   Vol. 1
   1. Spirituality
   I. Title II. Metamorphosen des Seelenlebens
   und Pfade der Seelenerlebnisse. *English*
   248.4   BV4501.2

ISBN 0-85440-414-7

Printed and bound in Great Britain at
The Camelot Press Ltd, Southampton

THE PUBLICATION OF LECTURES HELD BY RUDOLF STEINER

The foundation of anthroposophically orientated spiritual science is laid in the works which were written and published by Rudolf Steiner (1861-1925). At the same time Steiner held numerous lectures and courses both for the general public and for members of the Theosophical (later Anthroposophical) Society in the years between 1900 and 1924. It was not his original wish to have these lectures published which were without exception of a spontaneous nature and conceived as "oral communications not intended for print". However, after an increasing number of incomplete and erroneous listeners' transcripts had been printed and circulated, he found it necessary to have the notes regulated. He entrusted this task to Marie Steiner von Sivers. She was made responsible for the choice of stenographers, the supervision of their transcripts and the necessary revision of texts before publication. As Rudolf Steiner was only in a very few instances able to correct the notes himself his reservation in respect to all publications of his lectures must be taken into account: "Errors occurring in transcripts which I myself have been unable to revise will just have to be tolerated."

In Chapter 35 of his autobiography, Rudolf Steiner expounds on the relationship between his lectures for Members which were initially only circulated internally and his public writings. The relevant text is printed at the end of this volume. What is expressed there also applies to the lecture courses directed towards a restricted audience already familiar with the principles of spiritual science.

After Marie Steiner's death (1867-1948) the editing of a "Complete Works of Rudolf Steiner" was commenced according to her directions. The volume at hand constitutes a part of this complete edition. As far as necessary, particulars with regard to the text are to be found in the accompanying notes.

CONTENTS

Preface (from the 1983 German edition)   xii

Lecture 1. The Mission of Spiritual Science   1
Berlin, 14th October 1909.
The spirit is a reality for spiritual science. Count von Hoditz and Wolframitz, a personality of outstanding importance, said: Man is in essence an image of the Divine. Today spiritual science exists; a higher, supersensible form of knowledge. Goethe saw in the harmonious human being the goal of the universe. Kant denied a path of knowledge leading into the spiritual world, from which comes moral consciousness, duty and conscience. Goethe is his antithesis. By means of "contemplative judgement" one can ascend into the spiritual world. The stages on this path are Imagination, Inspiration and Intuition. Initiates in ancient times revealed the most profound secrets of life in legends and myths as well as in symbols. The "Therapeutae" were able to look into the spiritual world. Augustin experienced an awareness of the Divine. Today spiritual observation can be expressed in the logical terms of external science. It is the mission of spiritual science to ascend into the spiritual world by developing the hidden forces of the soul.

Lecture 2. The Mission of Anger   17
Munich, 5th December 1909.
There are hidden faculties in the soul. Soul and spirit can issue only from soul and spirit. The fact of repeated earth lives is a consequence of this. The sentient soul is connected with the sentient body, the Intellectual soul with the ether body and the consciousness soul with the physical body. In the sentient soul lie images, antipathy and sympathy. The intellectual soul forms thoughts and judgements with the outside world. We have to make ourselves as many-sided as possible and overcome egoism. Anger can educate the human being to calmness and true gentleness. Prometheus brought language, knowledge, writing and fire to mankind, all of them gifts which educate the ego. The wrath of Zeus extinguishes the power of the ego in Prometheus. Zeus is succeeded by Christ, anger by the loving ego.

vii

Lecture 3. The Mission of Truth   32
Berlin, 22nd October 1909.
The ego is confined between losing itself and egoism. Lessing demands that man strive for truth. A sense of truth leads to selflessness. The one-sided point of view does not lead to truth. Passions, desires, have to be overcome; to the same extent peace and harmony rules among man. There is the truth of reflective thought about outer observation, as well as truth which comes about by creative thought. Among the latter are the truths of spiritual science. Reflective thinking can lead to egoism; truths arrived at by creative thinking, which lead into the future, liberate us from our self. This is the contrast between Epimetheus and Prometheus. Both the Titan brothers must work together. Wisdom and the Word have to unite with the Deed.

Lecture 4. The Mission of Reverence   52
Berlin, 28th October 1909.
The "Unio mystica" is the union with the eternal-feminine within human reach. The human being should strengthen his ego but he must not harden it into egoism. The will is able to develop devotion towards the unknown, the feeling develops love for the unknown. When both are united reverence comes into being, which leads to knowledge of the unknown. Love without judgement leads to sentimental enthusiasm. Love and devotion imbued with the right kind of self-feeling lead upwards. Gestures of reverence are the bended knee, folded hands, the lifted face. The soul purifies within itself a feeling for what is beautiful and what is good. The will, purified by reverence, builds up moral ideals. In old age the strength arises to be active in life. We draw near to the Almighty. Increasingly rich knowledge is the result of educating the consciousness soul. The "eternal-masculine" must permeate all reverence. The strong ego ascends to higher regions.

Lecture 5. Human Character   64
Munich, 14th March 1909.
The divisions in the being of man must be overcome by the unified character. At its foundation lies the harmony brought forth by the ego from the interaction of the three soul members. The human being ripens through experience and wisdom learnt from life. Experiences are transformed into abilities. They are limited by the disposition of the physical and ether bodies. The forces which we have woven into archetype can only enter existence in a new life. The outer is an expression of the inner being. Laocoon, an image of the human being from which the ego is absent. True ripeness of experi-

Synopsis

ence is not attained until the 35th year of age. Joy and love fill the physical body of the child with strength. Then there are fewer obstacles for the ego in the period of the consciousness soul. Similar links exist between the ether body and the intellectual soul and the periods when they manifest themselves. The experience of authority in the period from 7 to 14 provides the foundation for courage. The ideals presented to the human being in the period from 14 to 21 are imprinted on the sentient soul. Immersion in the cosmic secrets further remoulds the character. Character is evident in facial expression, the physiognomy and the formation of the skull.

Lecture 6. Asceticism and Illness   80
    Berlin, 11th November 1909
Spiritual science asks how can the human being surpass the limits of his knowledge at a given time by developing his abilities. The human being requires the stimulus of the outside world for the development of his consciousness. But he can strengthen the inner members of his being in such a manner that he retains consciousness in them without stimulus from the outside world. A first exercise is symbolic concepts, such as the rose-cross. Such an exercise is asceticism in the true sense. The human being may reject the spiritual for reasons of self-preservation if it were to throw his mind into confusion. It would be self-destructive to accept knowledge of the spiritual world purely for sensationalism. It is the wrong type of asceticism to weaken the body and not work on the soul. False images of one's own being are the result. Illness can be a symptom for a faulty relationship between body and soul. By strengthening the forces of the soul healing forces can be given to the body.

Lecture 7. Human Egoism   98
    Berlin, 25th November 1909
For Goethe the human being is the summit of existence. The ego is the bearer of justified and unjustified egoism. If the human being places his experiences at the disposal of mankind he is a microcosm. If he does not do this, then he becomes hardened. The wrong kind of egoism leads to a desolate existence. All great truths have a health-giving effect on the soul. Feelings which develop understanding for the outer world strengthen the life-forces. Our strength of soul develops out of ourselves the world of our actions. In the human being the higher human being is born. Wisdom gained by insight into the world passes into the will. In "Wilhelm Meister" Goethe shows the nature of egoism. Mignon is a being which is not yet an ego. The "Beautiful Soul" initially shows a refined form of egoism. But then she experiences the course of Christ's life. The human being can understand the great world around him only when

Metamorphoses of the Soul

his own enriched inner being flows out into the environment. Spiritual forces guide the human being. In the "Years of Travel" various tales and much wisdom is interspersed. In the "pedagogical province" the significance of veneration is shown. Makarie experiences the universe. Self-knowledge can become world-knowledge and world knowledge can lead to self-knowledge.

Lecture 8. Buddha and Christ   119
Berlin, 2nd December 1909

Buddha speaks only about the means whereby man can come to an existence satisfying in itself. In the conversation between Nagasena and King Milinda the former shows how only effects pass from one earth-life to the next. Buddhism turns away from the physical world. The Christian carries the results of an earth-life into the next. Buddha sees the suffering which assails the human being from outside. The human being must fight the thirst for existence by means of the eight-fold path. Buddha wants release from the suffering of existence. Christianity is the religion of rebirth on a spiritual level. The East is non-historical, the West historical. Christianity sees the aim of development in that all the gains of earth-lives shine forth in ever higher levels of perfection and are resurrected at the end of earth-existence. It is Christian to overcome the error that the outside world is merely Maya. Everything which we experience in the incarnations must be developed in order that it may experience resurrection in the spiritual sense. At the time of Christ the old clairvoyance wanes. In its place the culture of the ego arises. The beatitudes point the way to the ego, to the divine part in the human being. The death of Christ is the starting-point for an immortal life. In the last instance Faust ascends from death to life. In Goethe a Christianity of the future appears.

Lecture 9. Something about the Moon   135
in the Light of Spiritual Science
Berlin, 9th December 1909

The "moon controversy" between Fechner and Schleiden. Fechner collated many observations on the rhythm of the moon. Goethe was working on meteorological studies. He sees the earth as a being imbued with life. The ego works on the three soul members. The sentient body is connected with man's place of home. The angle at which the sun's rays strike the earth varies from place to place. The ether body is dependent on the change of the seasons. In the far north and in the tropics the intellectual soul is unable to create a useful instrument from the ether body. The physical body develops in the alternation of day and night. Productive periods occur in 14-day rhythms. For the spiritual researcher there are periods when

Synopsis

spiritual illuminations surge in on him and others when he penetrates them with his thinking. The earth holds the moon in orbit. The forces of the moon work to prepare the bearers of the soul. The human being transforms the external rhythm into an internal one. The tides are caused by deeper forces in the earth. The embryonic period is determined by ten lunar months.

Notes   153

Concerning the Transcripts of the Lectures   158

PREFACE

The series of public lectures given in the Architect's House, Berlin, in 1909/1910 is being published in the 1983 edition in *chronological* order. In the first edition, on which all further editions so far have been based, Marie Steiner (who also chose the titles) arranged the *Metamorphoses of the Soul* and *Paths of Experience* according to criteria of contents. Three of the lectures (20th January, 3rd March and 28th April) were not included in the two volumes and were published elsewhere.

The lectures on 21st and 29th October were replaced right from the first edition by parallel lectures in Munich (5th December 1909 and 14th March 1910). The Berlin lecture on 21st October, "The Mission of Anger", is incomplete towards the end and the direction which the Munich lecture takes at the end in content is not present in the Berlin one. The lecture on 29th October, "Human Character", only became available to the Archive in the 1960's and the text is too fragmentary for it to replace the Munich parallel lecture, although in style it would fit better into the Berlin series of lectures. Of particular note is that the later Munich version develops aspects in compressed form which are presented in Berlin in two different contexts. Thus the Munich lecture contains aspects of the lectures "Human Character" and "Sickness and Healing" (3rd March 1910, 2nd vol.).

LECTURE 1
The Mission of Spiritual Science

Berlin, 14th October, 1909

This year I shall again be giving a series of lectures on subjects related to Spiritual Science, as I have done now for several years past. Those of my audience who attended those previous lectures will know what is meant here by the term, Spiritual Science (*Geisteswissenschaft*). For others, let me say that it will not be my task to discuss some abstract branch of science, but a discipline which treats the spirit as something actual and real. It starts from the premise that human experience is not unavoidably restricted to sense-perceptible reality or to the findings of human reason and other cognitive faculties in so far as they are bound up with the sense-perceptable. Spiritual Science says that it is possible for human beings to penetrate behind the realm of the sense-perceptible and to make observations which are beyond the range of the ordinary intellect.

This introductory lecture will describe the role of Spiritual Science in present-day life, and will show how in the past this Spiritual Science —which is as old as humanity—appeared in a form very different from the form it must take today. In speaking of the present, I naturally do not mean the immediate here and now, but the relatively long period during which spiritual life has had the particular character which has come to full development in our own time.

Anyone who looks back over the spiritual life of mankind will see that "a time of transition" is a phrase to be used with care, for every period can be so described. Yet there are times when spiritual life takes a leap forward, so to speak. From the 16th century onwards, the relationship between the soul and spiritual life of human beings and the outer world has been different from what it was in earlier times. And the further back we go in human evolution, the more we find that men had different needs, different longings, and gave different answers from within themselves to questions concerning the great riddles of existence.

Metamorphoses of the Soul

We can gain a clear impression of these transition periods through individuals who lived in those days and had retained certain qualities of feeling, knowing and willing from earlier periods, but were impelled to meet the demands of a new age.

Let us take an interesting personality and see what he makes of questions concerning the being of man and other such questions that must closely engage human minds—a personality who lived at the dawn of modern spiritual life and was endowed with the inner characteristics I have just described. I will not choose anyone familiar, but a sixteenth century thinker who was unknown outside a small circle. In his time there were many persons who retained, as he did, mediaeval habits of thinking and feeling and wished to gain knowledge in the way that had been followed for centuries, and yet were moving on towards the outlook of the coming age. I shall be naming an individual of whose external life almost nothing is historically known. From the point of view of Spiritual Science, this is thoroughly congenial. Anyone who has sojourned in the realm of Spiritual Science will know how distracting it is to find attached to a personality all the petty details of everyday life that are collected by modern biographers. On this account, we ought to be thankful that history has preserved so little about Shakespeare, for instance; the true picture is not spoilt—as it is with Goethe—by all the trivia the biographers are so fond of dragging in. I will therefore designate an individual of whom even less is known than is known about Shakespeare, a seventeenth century thinker who is of great significance for anyone who can see into the history of human thinking.

In Francis Joseph Philipp, Count von Hoditz and Wolframitz, who led the life of a solitary thinker during the second half of the seventeenth century in Bohemia, we have a personality of outstanding importance from this historical point of view. In a little work entitled *Libellus de nominis convenientia*[1]—I have not inquired if it has since been published in full—he set down the questions which occupied his soul. If we immerse ourselves in his soul, these questions can lead us into the issues that a reflecting man would concern himself with in those days. This lonely thinker discusses the great central problem of the being of man. With a forcefulness that springs from a deep need for knowledge, he says that nothing so disfigures a man as not to know what his being really is.

Count von Hoditz turns to important figures in the history of thought, for instance to Aristotle in the fourth century B.C., and asks what Aristotle says in answer to this question—what the essential being of man really is.[2] He says: Aristotle's answer is that man is a rational animal. Then he turns to a later thinker, Descartes, and puts the same

The Mission of Spiritual Science

question, and here the answer is that man is a thinking being.[3] But on reflection he comes to feel that these two representative thinkers can give no answer to his question; for—as he says—in the answers of Aristotle and Descartes he wanted to learn what man is and what he ought to do. When Aristotle says that man is a rational animal, that is no answer to the question of what man is, for it throws no light on the nature of rationality. Nor does Descartes in the seventeenth century tell us what man ought to do in accordance with his nature as a thinking being. For although we may know that man is a thinking being, we do not know what he must think in order to take hold of life in the right way, in order to relate his thought to life.

Thus our philosopher sought in vain for an answer to this vital question, a question that must be answered if a man is not to lose his bearings. At last he came upon something which will seem strange to a modern reader, especially if he is given to scientific ways of thought, but for our solitary thinker it was the only answer appropriate to the particular constitution of his soul. It was no help for him to know that man is a rational animal or a thinking being. At last he found his question answered by another thinker who had it from an old tradition. And he framed the answer he had thus discovered in the following words: Man in his essence is an image of the Divine.[4] Today we should say that man in his essence is what his whole origin in the spiritual world makes him to be.

The remaining remarks by Count von Hoditz need not occupy us today. All that concerns us is that the needs of his soul drove him to an answer which went beyond anything man can see in his environment or comprehend by means of his reason. If we examine the book more closely, we find that its author had no knowledge gained direct from the spiritual world. Now if he had been troubled by the question of the relation between sun and earth, he could, even if he were not an observer himself, have found the answer somewhere among the observations collected by the new forms of scientific thought. With regard to external questions of the sense-world he could have used answers given by people who had themselves investigated the questions through their own observations and experiences. But the experiences available to him at that time gave no answer to the questions concerning man's spiritual life, his real being in so far as it is spiritual. Clearly, he had no means of finding persons who themselves had had experiences in the spiritual world and so could communicate to him the properties of the spiritual world in the same way as the scientists could impart to him their knowledge about the external world. So he turned to religious tradition and its records. He certainly assimilated his findings—this is characteristic of his quality of soul—but one can see from the way he worked that he was only able to use his intellect to give a new form to what he had found emerging from the course of history or from recorded tradition.

Many people will now be inclined to ask: Are there—can there be—any persons who from their own observation and experience are able to answer questions related to the riddles of spiritual life?

This is precisely what Spiritual Science will make people aware of once more: the fact that—just as research can be carried out in the sense-perceptible world—it is possible to carry out research in the spiritual world, where no physical eyes, no telescopes or microscopes are available, and that answers can thus be given from direct experience as to conditions in such a world beyond the range of the senses. We shall then recognise that there was an epoch, conditioned by the whole evolutionary progress of humanity, when other means were used to make known the findings of spiritual research, and that we now have an epoch when these findings can once more be spoken of and understanding for them can again be found.

In between lay the twilight time of our solitary thinker, when human evolution took a rest, so to speak, from ascending towards the spiritual world, and preferred to rely on traditions passed down through ancient records or by word of mouth. In certain circles it began to be doubted whether it was possible for human beings to enter a spiritual world through their own powers by developing the cognitive faculties that lie hidden or slumbering within them. Are there, then, any rational grounds for saying that it is nonsensical to speak of a spiritual world that lies beyond the sense-perceptible? A glance at the progress of ordinary science should be enough to justify this question. Precisely a consideration of the wonderful advances that have been made in unravelling the secrets of external nature should indicate to anyone that a higher, supersensible knowledge must exist. How so?

If we study human evolution impartially, we cannot fail to be impressed by the exceptional progress made in recent times by the sciences concerned with the outer world. With what pride—and in a certain sense the pride is justified—do people remark that the vast, ever-increasing advance of modern science has brought to light many facts that were unknown a few centuries ago. For example, thousands of years ago the sun rose in the morning and passed across the heavens, just as it does today. That which could be seen in the surroundings of the earth and in connection with the course of the sun was the same then, for external observation, as it was in the days of Galileo, Newton, Kepler, Copernicus, and so on. But what could men say in those earlier ages about the external world? Can we suppose that the modern know-

The Mission of Spiritual Science

ledge of which we are so justly proud has been gained by merely contemplating the external world? If the external world could itself, just as it is, give us this knowledge, there would be no need to look further: all the knowledge we have about the sense-perceptible world would have been acquired centuries ago. How is it that we know so much more and have a different view of the position of the sun and so on? It is because human understanding, human cognition concerning the external world, has developed and changed in the course of hundreds or thousands of years. Yes, these faculties were by no means the same in ancient Greece as they have come to be with us since the 16th century.

Anyone who studies these changes without prejudice must say to himself: Men have acquired something new. They have learnt to see the outer world differently because of something added to those faculties which apply to the external sense-world. Hence it became clear that the sun does not revolve round the earth; these new faculties compelled men to think of the earth as going round the sun.

No-one who is proud of the achievements of physical science can have any doubt that in his inner being man is capable of development, and that his powers have been remodelled from stage to stage until he has become what he is to-day. But he is called upon to develop more than outer powers; he has in his inner life something which enables him to recreate the world in the light of his inward capacity for knowledge. Among the finest words of Goethe are the following (in his book about Winckelmann)[5]: "If the healthy nature of man works as a unity, if he feels himself within the world as in a great, beautiful, noble and worthy whole, if harmonious ease offers him a pure and free delight: then the universe, if it could become conscious of itself, would rise in exultation at having reached its goal and would stand in wonder at the climax of its own being and becoming." And again: "Man, placed at the summit of Nature, is again a whole new nature, which must in turn achieve a summit of its own. He ascends towards that height when he permeates himself with all perfections and virtues, summons forth order, selection, harmony and meaning, and attains in the end to the creation of a work of art."

So man can feel that he has been born out of the forces he can see with his eyes and grasp with his reason. But if he applies the unbiased observation we have mentioned, he will see that not only external Nature has forces which develop until they are observed by the human eye, heard by the human ear, grasped by the human reason. In the same way a study of human evolution will show that something evolves within man; the faculties for gaining exact knowledge of nature were at first asleep within him, and have awakened by stages in the course of

Metamorphoses of the Soul

time. Now they are fully awake, and it is these faculties which have made possible the great progress of physical science.

Is it then inevitable that these inner faculties should remain as they are now, equipped only to reflect the outer world? Is it not perfectly reasonable to ask whether the human soul may not possess other hidden powers that can be awakened? May it not be that if he develops further the powers that lie hidden and slumbering within him, they will be spiritually illuminated, so that his spiritual eye and spiritual ear— as Goethe calls them[6]—will be opened and will enable him to perceive a spiritual world behind the sense-world?

To anyone who follows this thought through without prejudice, it will not seem nonsensical that hidden forces should be developed to open the way into the supersensible world and to answer the questions: What is man in his real being? If he is an image of the spiritual world, what, then, is this spiritual world?

If we describe man in external terms and call to mind his gestures, instincts and so forth, we shall find all these characteristics represented imperfectly in lower beings. We shall see his external semblance as an integration of instincts, gestures and forces which are divided up among a number of lower creatures. We can comprehend this because we see around us the elements from which man has evolved into man. Might it not be possible then, to use these developed forces to penetrate similarly into a *spiritual* external world and to see there beings, forces and objects, just as we see stones, plants and animals in the physical world? Might it not be possible to observe spiritual processes which would throw light on man's inner life, just as it is possible to clarify his relationship to the outer world?

There has been, however, an interval between the old and the modern way of communicating Spiritual Science. This was a time of rest for the greater part of mankind. Nothing new was discovered; the old sources and traditions were worked over again and again. For the period in question this was quite right; every period has a characteristic way of meeting its fundamental needs. So this interlude occurred, and we must realise that while it lasted men were in a special situation, different both from what had been in the past and from what would be in the future. In a certain sense they became unaccustomed to looking for the soul's hidden faculties, which could have given insight into the spiritual world. So a time drew on when men could no longer believe or understand that the inner development of hidden faculties leads to supersensible knowledge. Even then, one fact could hardly be denied: that in human beings there is something invisible. For how could it be thought that human reason, for example, is a visible entity? What sort

The Mission of Spiritual Science

of impartial thinking could fail to admit that human cognition is by its nature a supersensible faculty?

Knowledge of this fact was never quite lost, even in the time when men had ceased to believe that supersensible faculties within the soul could be developed so as to give access to the supersensible. One particular thinker reduced this faculty to its smallest limit: it was impossible, he said, for men to penetrate by supersensible vision into a world that comes objectively before us as a spiritual world, just as animals, plants and minerals and other people are encountered in the physical world. Yet even he had to recognise impartially that something supersensible does exist and cannot be denied.

This thinker was Kant,[7] who thus brought an earlier phase of human evolution to a certain conclusion. For what does he think about man's relationship to a supersensible, spiritual world? He does not deny that a man observes something supersensible when he looks into himself, and that for this purpose he employs faculties of knowledge which cannot be perceived by physical eyes, however far the refinement of our physical instruments may be carried. Kant, then, does point to something supersensible; the faculties used by the soul to make for itself a picture of the outer world. But he goes on to say that this is all that can be known concerning a supersensible world. His opinion is that wherever a man may turn his gaze, he sees only this one thing he can call supersensible: the supersensible element contained in his senses in order that he may perceive and grasp and understand the existence of the sense-world.

In the Kantian philosophy, accordingly, there is no path that can lead to observation or experience of the spiritual world. The one thing Kant admits is the possibility of recognising that knowledge of the external world cannot be attained by the senses, but only by supersensible means. This is the sole experience of the supersensible that man can have.

That is the historically important feature of Kant's philosophy. But in Kant's argument it cannot be denied that when man uses his thinking in connection with his actions and deeds, he has the means to affect the sense-perceptible world. Thus, Kant had to recognise that a human being does not follow only instinctive impulses, as lower animals do; he also follows impulses from within his soul, and these can raise him far above subservience to mere instinct. There are countless examples of people who are tempted by a seductive impulse to do something, but they resist the temptation and take as their guide to action something that cannot come from an external stimulus. We need only think of the great martyrs, who gave up everything the sense-world could offer for something that was to lead them beyond the sense-world. Or we need only point to the experience of conscience in the human soul, even in the Kantian sense. When a man encounters something ever so charming and tempting, conscience can tell him not to be lured away by it, but to follow the voice that speaks to him from spiritual depths, an indomitable voice within his soul. And so for Kant it was certain that in man's inner being there is such a voice, and that what it says cannot be compared with any message from the outer world. Kant called it the categorical imperative—a significant phrase. But he goes on to say that man can get no further than this voice from the soul as a means of acting on the world from out of the supersensible, for he cannot rise beyond the world of the senses. He feels that duty, the categorical imperative, conscience, speak from within him, but he cannot penetrate into the realm from which they come.

Kant's philosophy allows man to go no further than the boundary of the supersensible world. Everything else that resides in the realm from which duty, conscience and the categorical imperative emanate is shut off from observation, although it is of the same supersensible nature as the soul. Man cannot enter that realm; at most he can draw conclusions about it. He can say to himself: Duty speaks to me, but I am weak; in the ordinary world I cannot carry out fully the injunctions of duty and conscience. Therefore I must accept the fact that my being is not confined to the world of the senses, but has a significance beyond that world. I can hold this before me as a belief, but it is not possible for me to penetrate into the world beyond the senses; the world from which come the voices of moral consciousness, duty and conscience, the categorical imperative.

We will now turn to someone who in this context was the exact antithesis of Kant: I mean Goethe. Anyone who truly compares the souls of these two men will see that they are diametrically opposed in their attitudes towards the most important problems of knowledge. Goethe, after absorbing all that Kant had to say about these problems, maintained on the ground of his own inner experience that Kant was wrong. Kant, says Goethe, claims that man has the power to form intellectual, conceptual judgments, but is not endowed with any contemplative faculty which could give direct experience of the spiritual world. But—Goethe continues—anyone who has exercised himself with the whole force of his personality to wrest his way from the sense-world to the supersensible, as I have done, will know that we are not limited to drawing conclusions, but through a contemplative power of judgement we are able actually to raise ourselves into the spiritual world. Such was Goethe's personal reply to Kant. He emphasises that anyone

The Mission of Spiritual Science

who asserts the existence of this contemplative judgement is embarking on an adventure of reason, but he adds that from his own experience he has courageously gone through this adventure![8]

Yet in the recognition of what Goethe calls "contemplative judgement" lies the essence of Spiritual Science, for it leads, as Goethe knew, into a spiritual world; and it can be developed, raised to ever higher levels, so as to bring about direct vision, immediate experience, of that world. The fruits of this enhanced intuition are the content of true Spiritual Science. In coming lectures we shall be concerned with these fruits: with the results of a science which has its source in the development of hidden faculties in the human soul, for they enable man to gaze into a spiritual world, just as through the external instruments of the senses he is able to gaze into the realms of chemistry and physics.

It could now be asked: Does this possibility of developing hidden faculties that slumber in the soul belong only to our time, or has it always existed?

A study of the course of human history from a spiritual-scientific point of view teaches us that there existed ancient stores of wisdom, parts of which were condensed into those writings and traditions which survived during the intermediate period I described earlier. This same Spiritual Science also shows us that today it is again possible not merely to proclaim the old, but to speak of what the human soul can itself achieve by development of the forces and faculties slumbering within it; so that a healthy judgment, even where human beings cannot themselves see into the spiritual world, can understand the findings of the spiritual researcher. The contemplative judgment that Goethe had in mind when he spoke out against Kant, is in a certain sense the beginning of the upward path of knowledge which today is by no means unexplored. Spiritual Science is therefore able to show, as we shall see, that there are hidden faculties of knowledge which by ascending order penetrate ever further into the spiritual world.

When we speak of knowledge, we generally mean knowledge of the ordinary world, "material knowledge"; but we can also speak of "imaginative knowledge", "inspired knowledge" and finally "intuitive knowledge".[9] These are stages of the soul's progress into the supersensible world which are also experienced by the individual spiritual researcher in accord with the constitution of the soul today. Similar paths were followed by the spiritual researcher in times gone by. But spiritual research has no meaning if it is to remain the possession of a few; it cannot limit itself to a small circle. Certainly, anything an ordinary scientist has to say about the nature of plants or about processes in the animal world can be of service to all mankind, even though this knowledge is actually possessed by a small circle of botanists, zoologists and so on. But spiritual research is not like that. It has to do with the needs of every human soul; with questions related to the inmost joys and sorrows of the soul; with knowledge that enables the human being to endure his destiny, and in such a way that he experiences inner contentment and bliss even if destiny brings him sorrow and suffering. If certain questions remain unanswered, men are left desolate and empty, and precisely they are the concern of Spiritual Science. They are not questions that can be dealt with only in restricted circles; they concern us all, at whatever stage of development and culture we may be, for the answering of them is spiritual food for each and every soul.

This has always been so, at all times. And if Spiritual Science is to speak to mankind in this way, it must find means of making itself understood by all who wish to understand it. This entails that it must direct itself to those powers which are most fully developed during a given period, so that they can respond to what the spiritual researcher has to impart. Since human nature changes from epoch to epoch and the soul is always acquiring new aptitudes, it is natural that in the past Spiritual Science should have spoken differently about the most burning questions that concern the soul. In remote antiquity it spoke to a humanity which would never have understood the way it speaks today, for the soul-forces which have now developed were non-existent then. If Spiritual Science had been presented in the way appropriate for the present day, it would have been as though one were talking to plants.

In ancient times, accordingly, the spiritual researcher had to use other means. And if we look back into remote antiquity, Spiritual Science itself tells us that in order to give answers in a form adapted to the soul-powers of mankind in those times, a different preparation was necessary for those who were training themselves to gaze into the spiritual world; they had to cultivate powers other than those needed for speaking to present-day mankind.

Men who develop the forces that slumber in the soul in order to gaze into the spiritual world and to see spiritual beings there, as we see stones, plants and animals in the physical world—these men are and always have been called by Spiritual Science, Initiates, and the experiences that the soul has to undergo in order to achieve this faculty is called Initiation. But in the past the way to it was different from what it is today, for the mission of Spiritual Science is always changing. The old Initiation, which had to be gone through by those who had to speak to the people in ancient times, led them to an immediate experience of the spiritual world. They could see into surrounding realms which are

The Mission of Spiritual Science

higher than those perceived through the senses. But they had to transform what they saw into symbolic pictures, so that people could understand it. Indeed, it was only in pictures that the old Initiates could express what they had seen, but these pictures embraced everything that could interest people in those days.

These pictures, drawn from real experience, are preserved for us in myths and legends which have come down from the most diverse periods and peoples. In academic circles these myths and legends are attributed to the popular imagination. Those who are cognisant of the facts know that myths and legends derive from supersensible vision, and that in every genuine myth and legend we must see an externalised picture of something a spiritual researcher has experienced, or, in Goethe's words, what he has seen with the spiritual eye or heard with the spiritual ear. We come to understand legends and myths only when we take them as images expressing a real knowledge of the spiritual world. They are pictures through which the widest circles of people could be reached.

It is a mistake to assume—as it so often is nowadays—that the human soul has always been just as it is in our century. The soul has changed; its receptivity was quite different in the past. A person was satisfied then if he received the picture given in the myth, for he was inspired by the picture to bring an intuitive vision of the outer world much more directly before his soul. Today myths are regarded as fantasy; but when in former times the myth sank into a person's soul, secrets of human nature were shown to him. When he looked at the clouds or the sun and so forth, he understood as a matter of course what the myth had set before him. In this way something we could call higher knowledge was given to a minority in symbolic form. While to-day we talk and must talk in straightforward language, it would be impossible to express in our terms what the souls of the old sages or initiates received, for neither the initiates nor their hearers had the soul-forces we have now developed.

In those early times the only valid forms of expression were pictorial. These pictures are preserved in a literature which strikes a modern reader as very strange. Now and then, especially if one is prompted by curiosity as well as by a desire for knowledge, one comes across an old book containing remarkable pictures which show, for example, the interconnections between the planets, together with all sorts of geometrical figures, triangles, polygons and so on. Anyone who applies a modern intellect to these pictures, without having acquired a special taste for them, will say: What can one do with all this stuff, the so-called Key of Solomon[10] as a traditional symbol, these triangles and polygons and such-like?

Certainly, the spiritual researcher will agree that from the standpoint of modern culture nothing can be made of all this. But when the pictures were first given to students, something in their souls really was aroused. Today the human soul is different. It has had to develop in such a way as to give modern answers to questions about nature and life, and so it cannot respond in the old way to such things as two interlocked triangles, one pointing upwards, the other downwards. In former times, this picture could kindle an active response; the soul gazed into it and something emerging from within it was perceived. Just as nowadays the eye can look through a microscope and see, for example, plant-cells that cannot be seen without it, so did these symbolic figures serve as instruments for the soul. A man who held the Key of Solomon as a picture before his soul could gain a glimpse of the spiritual world. With our modern souls this is not possible, and so the secrets of the spiritual world which are handed down in these old writings can no longer be knowledge in the original sense, and those who give them out as knowledge, or who did so in the 19th century, are doing something out of line with the facts. That is why one cannot do anything with writings such as those of Eliphas Levi, [11] for instance, for in our time it is antiquated to present these symbols as purporting to throw light on the spiritual world. In earlier times, however, it was proper for Spiritual Science to speak to the human soul through the powerful pictures of myth and legend, or alternatively through symbols of the kind I have just described.

Then came the intermediate period, when knowledge of the spiritual world was handed down from one generation to the next in writing or by oral tradition. Even if we study only external history, we can readily see how it was handed down. In the very early days of Christianity there was a sect in North Africa called the Therapeutae[12] : a man who had been initiated into their knowledge said that they possessed the ancient writings of their founders, who could still see into the spiritual world. Their successors could receive only what these writings had to say, or at most what could be discerned in them by those who had achieved some degree of spiritual development.

If we pass on to the Middle Ages, we find certain outstanding persons saying: we have certain cognitive faculties, we have reason; then, beyond ordinary reason we have faculties which can rise to a comprehension of certain secrets of existence; but there are other secrets and mysteries of existence which are only accessible by revelation. They are beyond the range of faculties which can be developed, they can be searched for only in ancient writings.

The Mission of Spiritual Science

Hence arose the great mediaeval split between those things that can be known by reason and those that must be believed because they are passed down by tradition, are revelation.[13] And it was quite in keeping with the outlook of those times that the frontier between reason and faith should be clearly marked. This was justified for that period, for the time had passed when certain mathematical signs could be used to call forth faculties of cognition in the human soul. Right up to modern times, a person had only one means of grasping the supersensible: looking into his own soul, as Augustine,[14] for example, did to some extent.

It was no longer possible to see in the outer world anything that revealed deep inner secrets. Symbols had come to be regarded as mere fantasies. One thing only survived: a recognition that the supersensible world corresponded to the supersensible in man, so that a man could say to himself: You are able to think, but your thought is limited by space and time, while in the spiritual world there is a Being who is pure thought. You have a limited capacity for love, whereas in the spiritual world there is a Being who is perfect love. When the spiritual world was represented for a human being in terms of his own inner experience, his inner life could extend to a vision of nature permeated by the Divine; then he had consciousness of God. But for particular facts he could turn only to information given in ancient writings, for in himself he had nothing that could lead him into the spiritual world.

Then came the later times which brought the proud achievements of natural science. These are the times when faculties which could go beyond the sense-perceptible emerged not only in those who achieved scientific knowledge, but in all men. Something in the soul came to understand that the picture given to the senses is not the real thing, and to realise that truth and appearance are contraries. This new faculty, which is able to discern outward nature in a form not given to the senses, will be increasingly understood by those who today penetrate as researchers into the spiritual world and are then able to report that one can see a spiritual world and spiritual beings, just as down here in the sense-perceptible world one sees animals, plants and minerals.

Hence the spiritual researcher has to speak of realms which are not far removed from present-day understanding. And we shall see how the symbols which were once a means for gaining knowledge of the spiritual world have become an aid to spiritual development. The Key of Solomon, for instance, which once called forth in the soul a real spiritual perception, does so no longer. But if today the soul allows itself to be acted on by what the spiritual researcher can explain concerning this symbol, something in the soul is aroused, and this can lead a person on by stages into

Metamorphoses of the Soul

the spiritual world. Then, when he has gained vision of the spiritual world, he can express what he has seen in the same logical terms that apply to external science.

Spiritual Science or occultism must therefore speak in a way that can be grasped by anyone who has a broad enough understanding. Whatever the spiritual researcher has to impart must be clothed in the conceptual terms which are customary in other sciences, or due regard would not be paid to the needs of the times. Not everyone can see immediately into the spiritual world, but since the appropriate forces of reason and feeling are now existent in every soul, Spiritual Science, if rightly presented, can be grasped by every normal person with his ordinary reason. The spiritual researcher is now again in a position to present what our solitary thinker said to himself: Man in his essence is an image of the Godhead.

If we want to understand the physical nature of man, we look to the relevant findings of physical research. If we want to understand his inner spiritual being, we look to the realm which the spiritual researcher is able to investigate. Then we see that man does not come into existence at birth or at conception, only to pass out of existence at death, but that besides the physical part of his organism he has super-sensible members. If we understand the nature of these members, we penetrate into the realm where faith passes over into knowledge. And when Kant, in the evening of an older period, said that we can recognise the categorical imperative, but that no-one can penetrate with conscious vision into the realm of freedom, of divine being and immortality, he was expressing only the experience natural to his time. Spiritual Science will show that we can penetrate into a spiritual world; that just as the eye equipped with a microscope can penetrate into realms beyond the range of the naked eye, so can the soul equipped with the means of Spiritual Science penetrate into an otherwise inaccessible spiritual world, where love, conscience, freedom and immortality can be known, even as we know animals, plants and minerals in the physical world. In subsequent lectures we will go further into this.

If once more we look now at the relationship between the spiritual researcher and his public, and at the difference between the past and present of Spiritual Science, we can say: The symbolic pictures used by spiritual researchers in the past acted directly on the human soul, because what today we call the faculties of reason and understanding were not yet present. The pictures gave direct vision of the spiritual world, and the ordinary man could not test with his reason what the spiritual researcher communicated to him through them. The pictures acted with the force of suggestion, of inspiration; a man subjected to

The Mission of Spiritual Science

them was carried away and could not resist them. Anyone who was given a false picture was thus delivered over to those who gave it to him. Therefore, in those early times it was of the utmost importance that those who rose into the spiritual world should be able to inspire absolute confidence and firm belief in their trustworthiness; for if they misused their power they had in their hands an instrument which they could exploit in the worst possible way.

Hence in the history of Spiritual Science there are periods of degeneration as well as times of brilliance; times in which the power of untrustworthy initiates was misused. How the initiate in those early times behaved towards his public depended to the utmost degree on himself alone. At the present time—and one might say, thank God for it!—all this is somewhat different. Since the change does not come about all at once, it is still necessary that the initiate should be a trustworthy person, and it will then be justified to feel every confidence in him. But people are already in a different relationship to the spiritual researcher; if he is to speak in accordance with the demands of his time he must speak in such a way that every unbiassed mind can understand him, if the willingness to understand him is there. This is, of course, far removed from saying that everyone who could understand must now understand. But reason can now be the judge of what an individual can understand, and therefore everyone who devotes himself to Spiritual Science should bring his unbiassed judgment to bear on it.

From now onwards this will be the mission of Spiritual Science: to rise into a spiritual world, through the development of hidden powers, just as the physiologist penetrates through the microscope into a realm of the smallest entities, invisible to the naked eye. And ordinary intelligence will be able to test the findings of spiritual research, as it can test the findings of the physiologist, the botanist, and so on. A healthy intelligence will be able to say of the spiritual researcher's findings: they are all consistent with one another. Modern man will come to the point of saying to himself: My reason tells me that it can be so , and by using my reason I can grasp clearly what the spiritual researcher has to tell. And that is how the spiritual researcher, for his part, should speak if he feels himself to be truly at one with the mission of Spiritual Science at the present time. But there will be a time of transition also today. For since the means to achieve spiritual development are available and can be used wrongly, many people whose purpose is not pure, whose sense of duty is not sacred and whose conscience is not infallible, will find their way into a spiritual world. But then, instead of behaving like a spiritual researcher who can know from his own experience whether the things he sees are in accord with the facts, these pretended

Metamorphoses of the Soul

researchers will impart information that goes against the facts. Moreover, since people can come only by slow degrees to apply their reasoning powers to understanding what the spiritual researcher says, we must expect that charlatanry, humbug and superstition will flourish pre-eminently in this realm. But the situation is changing. Man now has himself to blame if, without wishing to use his intellect, he is led by a certain curiosity to believe blindly in those who pass themselves off as spiritual investigators, so-called. Because men are too comfort-loving to apply their reason, and prefer a blind faith to thinking for themselves, it is possible that nowadays we may have, instead of the old initiate who misused his power, the modern charlatan who imposes on people not the truth, but something he perhaps takes for truth. This is possible because today we are at the beginning of an evolutionary phase.

There is nothing to which a man should apply his reason more rigorously than the communications that can come to him from Spiritual Science. People can lay part of the blame on themselves if they fall victim to charlatanry and humbug; for these falsities will bear abundant fruit, as indeed they have done already in our time. This is something that must not go unnoticed when we are speaking of the mission of Spiritual science today.

Anyone who listens now to a spiritual researcher—not in a wilful, negative way that casts immediate doubt on everything, but with a readiness to test everything in the light of healthy reason—will soon feel how Spiritual Science can bring hope and consolation in difficult hours, and can throw light on the great riddles of existence. He will come to feel that these riddles and the great questions of destiny can be resolved through Spiritual Science; he will come to know what part of him is subject to birth and death, and what is the eternal core of his being. In brief, it will be possible—as we shall show in later lectures—that, given good will and the wish to strengthen himself by taking in and working over inwardly the communications of Spiritual Science, he will be able to say with deepest feeling: What Goethe divined and said in his youth is true, and so are the lines he wrote in his maturity and gave to Faust to speak:

> The spirit world is ever open,
> Dead is thy heart, thy sense-veil closely drawn!
> Up, scholar, let thy breast unwearied
> Bathe in the roseate hues of dawn![15]

In the dawn-lines of the *Spirit*!

LECTURE 2
The Mission of Anger

Munich, 5th December, 1909

When we penetrate more deeply into the human soul and consider its nature from the point of view here intended, we are repeatedly reminded of the ancient saying by the Greek sage, Heraclitus[16]: "Never will you find the boundaries of the soul, by whatever paths you search ; so all-embracing is the soul's being." We shall be speaking here of the soul and its life, not from the standpoint of contemporary psychology, but from that of Spiritual Science. Spiritual Science stands firmly for the real existence of a spiritual world behind all that is revealed to the senses and through them to the mind. It regards this spiritual world as the source and foundation of external existence and holds that the investigation of it lies within the reach of man.

In lectures given here, the difference between Spiritual Science and the many other standpoints of the present day has often been brought out; and need be mentioned only briefly now. In ordinary life and in ordinary science it is habitually assumed that human knowledge has certain boundaries and that the human mind cannot know anything beyond them. Spiritual Science holds that these boundaries are no more than temporary. They can be extended; faculties hidden in the soul can be called forth, and then, just as a man born blind who gains his sight through an operation emerges from darkness into a world of light and colour, so it is with a person whose hidden faculties awake. He will break through into a spiritual world which is always around us but cannot be directly known until the appropriate spiritual organs for perceiving it have been developed. Spiritual Science asks: How are we to transform ourselves in order to penetrate into this world and to gain a comprehensive experience of it? And Spiritual Science must ever and again point to the great event which enables a man to become a spiritual investigator and so to direct his gaze into the spiritual worlds, even as a physicist sees into the physical world through his microscope. Goethe's words are certainly valid in their bearing on the spiritual world:

> Secretly, in the light of day,
> Nature's veil may not be lifted.
> What'er to your inquiring *spirit*
> She will not freely reveal,
> You cannot forcibly extract it,
> Not with levers, not with screws.[17]

Of course, the investigator in the sense of Spiritual Science has no such instrumental aids. He has to transform his soul into an instrument; then he experiences that great moment when his soul is awakened and the spiritual world around him reveals itself to his perception. Again, it has often been emphasised here that not everyone needs to be a spiritual investigator in order to appreciate what the awakened man has to impart. When knowledge resulting from spiritual research is communicated, no more is required of the listener than ordinary logic and an unbiased sense of truth. Investigation calls for the opened eye of the clairvoyant; recognition of what is communicated calls for a healthy sense of truth; natural feeling unclouded by prejudice; natural good sense. The point is that teachings and observations concerning the soul should be understood in the light of this spiritual research when in later lectures we come to speak of some of the humanly interesting characteristics of the soul. Just as anyone who wants to study hydrogen or oxygen or any other chemical substance has to acquire certain capabilities, so is observation of the life of the soul possible only for someone whose spiritual eye has been opened. The investigator of the soul must be in a position to make observations in soul-substance, so to speak. We must certainly not think of the soul as something vague and nebulous in which feelings, thoughts and volitions are whirling about. Let us rather remind ourselves of what has been said on this subject in previous lectures.

Man, as he stands before us, is a far more complicated being than he is held to be by exoteric science. For Spiritual Science, the knowledge drawn from external physical observation covers only a part of man—the external physical body which he has in common with all his mineral surroundings. Here, the same laws apply as in the external physical-mineral world, and the same substances function. As a result of observation, however, and not on the strength merely of logical inference, Spiritual Science recognises, beyond the physical body, a second member of man's being: we call it the etheric body or life-body. Only a brief reference can here be made to the etheric body—our task today is

The Mission of Anger

quite different—but knowledge of the underlying members of the human organism is the foundation on which we have to build. Man has an etheric body in common with everything that lives. As I said, only the spiritual investigator, who has transformed his soul into an instrument for seeing into the spiritual world, can directly observe the etheric body. But its existence can be acknowledged by a healthy sense of truth, unclouded by contemporary prejudices. Take the physical body: it harbours the same physical and chemical laws that prevail in the external physical-mineral world. When are these physical laws revealed to us? When we have before us a lifeless human being. When a human being has passed through the gate of death, we see what the laws that govern the physical body really are. They are the laws that lead to the decomposition of the physical body; their effect on it is now quite different from their action during life. They are always present in the physical body; the reason why the living body does not obey them is that during life an antagonist of dissolution, the etheric or life-body, is also present and active there.

A third member of the human organism can now be distinguished: the vehicle of pleasure and pain, of urges, desires and passions—of everything we associate with the emotional activities of the soul. Man has this vehicle in common with all beings who possess a certain form of consciousness: with the animals. Astral body, or body of consciousness, is the name we give to this third member of the human organism.

This completes what we may call the bodily nature of man, with its three components: physical body, etheric body or life-body, astral or consciousness-body.

Within these three members we recognise something else; something unique to man, through which he has risen to the summit of creation. It has often been remarked that our language has one little word which guides us directly to man's inner being, whereby he ranks as the crown of earthly creation. These flowers here, the desk, the clock—anyone can name these objects; but there is one word we can never hear spoken by another with reference to ourselves; it must spring from our own inner being. This is the little name 'I'. If you are to call yourself 'I', this 'I' must sound forth from within yourself and must designate your inmost being. Hence the great religions and philosophies have always regarded this name as the 'unspeakable name' of that which cannot be designated from outside. Indeed, with this designation 'I', we stand before that innermost being of man which can be called the divine element in him. We do not thereby make man a god. If we say that a drop of water from the sea is of like substance with the ocean, we are not making the drop into a sea. Similarly, we are not making the 'I' a god when we say it is of like substance with the divine being that permeates and pulses through the world.

Through his inner essence, man is subject to a certain phenomenon which Spiritual Science treats as real and serious in the full sense of the words. Its very name fascinates people today, but in its application to man it is given full rank and worth only by Spiritual Science. It is the fact of existence that we call 'evolution'. How fascinating is the effect of this word on modern man, who can point to lower forms of life which evolve gradually into higher stages; how enchanting when it can be said that man himself has evolved from those lower forms to his present height! Spiritual Science takes evolution seriously in relation, above all, to man. It calls attention to the fact that man, since he is a self-conscious being with an inner activity springing from the centre of his being, should not limit his idea of evolution to a mere observation of the imperfect developing towards the more nearly perfect. As an active being he must himself take hold of his own evolution. He must raise himself to higher stages than the stage he has already reached; he must develop ever-new forces, so that he may approach continually towards perfection. Spiritual Science takes a sentence, first formulated not very long ago, and now recognised as valid in another realm, and applies it on a higher level to human evolution. Most people today are not aware that as late as the beginning of the 17th century the learned as well as the laity believed that the lower animals were born simply out of river-mud. This belief arose from imprecise observation, and it was the great natural scientist, Francesco Redi,[18] who in the 17th century first championed the statement: Life can arise only from the living. Naturally, this statement is quoted here in the modern sense, with all necessary qualifications. No-one, of course, now believes that any lower animal—say an earth-worm—can grow out of river-mud. For an earth-worm to come into existence, the germ of an earth-worm must first be there. And yet, in the 17th century, Francesco Redi narrowly escaped the fate of Giordano Bruno,[19] for his statement had made him a terrible heretic.

This sort of treatment is not usually inflicted on heretics to-day, at least not in all parts of the world, but there is a modern substitute for it. If anyone upholds something which contradicts the belief of those who, in their arrogance, suppose they have reached the summit of earthly wisdom, he is looked on as a visionary, a dreamer, if nothing worse. That is the contemporary form of inquisition in our parts of the world. Be it so. Nevertheless, what Spiritual Science says concerning phenomena on higher levels will come to be accepted equally with Francesco Redi's statement regarding the lower levels. Even as he asser-

The Mission of Anger

ted that "life can issue only from the living", so does Spiritual Science state that "soul and spirit can issue only from soul and spirit". And the law of reincarnation, so often ridiculed today as the outcome of crazy fantasy, is in fact a consequence of this statement. Nowadays, when people see, from the first day of a child's birth, the soul and spirit developing out of the bodily element; when they see increasingly definite facial traits emerging from an undifferentiated physiognomy, movements becoming more and more individual, talents and abilities showing forth—many people still believe that all this springs from the physical existence of father, mother, grandparents; in short, from physical ancestry.

This belief derives from inexact observation, just as did the belief that earth-worms originate from mud. Present-day sense-observation is incapable of tracing back to its soul-spiritual origin the soul and spirit that are manifest before our eyes today. Hence the laws of physical heredity are made to account for phenomena which apparently emerge from the obscure depths of the physical. Spiritual Science looks back to previous lives on earth, when the talents and characteristics that are evident in the present life were foreshadowed. And we regard the present life as the source of new formative influences that will bear fruit in future earthly lives.

Francesco Redi's statement has now become an obvious truth, and the time is not far distant when the corresponding statement by Spiritual Science will be regarded as equally self-evident—with the difference that Francesco Redi's statement is of restricted interest, while the statement by Spiritual Science concerns everyone: "Soul and spirit develop from soul and spirit; man does not live once only but passes through repeated lives on earth; every life is the result of earlier lives and the starting-point of numerous subsequent lives." All confidence in life, all certainty in our work, the solution of all the riddles facing us—it all depends on this knowledge. From this knowledge man will draw ever-increasing strength for his existence, together with confidence and hope when he looks towards the future.

Now what is it that originates in earlier lives, works on from life to life, and maintains itself through all its sojourns on earth? It is the Ego, the 'I', designated by the name which a person can bestow on no-one but himself. The human Ego goes from life to life, and in so doing fulfils its evolution.

But how is this evolution brought about? By the Ego working on the three lower members of the human being. We have first the astral body, the vehicle of pleasure and pain, of joy and sorrow, of instinct, desire and passion. Let us look at a person on a low level, whose Ego

Metamorphoses of the Soul

has done little, as yet, to cleanse his astral body and so is still its slave. In a person who stands higher we find that his Ego has worked upon his astral body in such a way that his lower instincts, desires and passions have been transmuted into moral ideals, ethical judgments. From this contrast we can gain a first impression of how the Ego works upon the astral body.

In every human being it is possible to distinguish the part of the astral body on which the Ego has not yet worked from the part which the Ego has consciously transformed. The transmuted part is called Spirit-Self, or Manas. The Ego may grow stronger and stronger and will then transmute the etheric body or life-body. Life-spirit is the name we give to the transformed etheric body. Finally, when the Ego acquires such strength that it is able to extend its transforming power into the physical body, we call the transmuted part Atma, or the real Spirit-man.

So far we have been speaking of conscious work by the Ego. In the far-distant past, long before the Ego was capable of this conscious work, it worked unconsciously—or rather sub-consciously—on the three bodies or sheaths of man. The astral body was the first to be worked on in this way, and its transmuted part we call the Sentient Soul, the first of man's soul-members. So it was that the Ego, working from the inner being of man, created the Sentient Soul at a time when man lacked the requisite degree of consciousness for transmuting his instincts, desires and so forth. In the etheric body the Ego created unconsciously the Mind-Soul or Intellectual Soul. Again, working unconsciously on the physical body, the Ego created the inner soul-organ that we call the Consciousness Soul. For Spiritual Science, the human soul is not a vague, nebulous something, but an essential part of man's being, consisting of three distinct soul-members—Sentient Soul, Mind-Soul, Consciousness Soul—within which the Ego is actively engaged.

Let us try to form an idea of these three soul-members. The spiritual investigator knows them by direct observation, but we can approach them also by means of rational thinking. For example, suppose we have a rose before us. We perceive it, and as long as we perceive it we are receiving an impression from outside. We call this a perception of the rose. If we turn our eyes away, an inner image of the rose remains with us. We must carefully distinguish these two moments: the moment when we are looking at the rose and the moment when we are able to retain an image of it as an inner possession, although we are no longer perceiving it.

This point must be emphasised because of the incredible notions brought forward in this connection by 19th century philosophy. We

The Mission of Anger

need think only of Schopenhauer,[20] whose philosophy begins with the words: The world is my idea. Hence we must be clear as to the difference between percepts and concepts, or mental images. Every sane man knows the difference between the concept of white-hot steel, which cannot burn him, and white-hot steel itself, which can. Perceptions bring us into communication with the external world; concepts are a possession of the soul. The boundary between inner experience and the outer world can be precisely drawn. Directly we begin to experience something inwardly, we owe it to the Sentient Soul—as distinct from the sentient body, which brings us our percepts and enables us to perceive, for example, the rose and its colour. Thus our concepts are formed in the Sentient Soul, and the Sentient Soul is the bearer also of our sympathies and antipathies, of the feelings that things arouse in us. When we call the rose beautiful, this inward experience is a property of the Sentient Soul.

Anyone who is unwilling to distinguish percepts from concepts should remember the white-hot steel that burns and the concept of it, which does not. Once, when I had said this, someone objected that a man might be able to suggest to himself the thought of lemonade so vividly that he would experience its taste on his tongue. I replied: Certainly this might be possible, but whether the imaginary lemonade would quench his thirst is another question. The boundary between external reality and inner experience can indeed always be determined. Directly inner experience begins, the Sentient Soul, as distinct from the sentient body, comes into play.

A higher principle is brought into being by the work of the Ego on the etheric body: we call it the Mind-Soul, or Intellectual Soul. We shall have more to say about it in the lecture on the Mission of Truth; today we are concerned especially with the Sentient Soul. Through the Intellectual Soul man is enabled to do more than carry about with him the experiences aroused in him by his perceptions of the outer world. He takes these experiences a stage further. Instead of merely keeping his perceptions alive as images in the Sentient Soul, he reflects on them and devotes himself to them; they form themselves into thoughts and judgments, into the whole content of his mind. This continued cultivation of impressions received from the outer world is the work of what we call the Intellectual Soul or Mind-soul.

A third principle is brought into being when the Ego has created in the physical body the organs whereby it is enabled to go out from itself and to connect its judgments, ideas and feelings with the external world. This principle we call the Consciousness Soul, because the Ego is then able to transform its inner experiences into conscious knowledge of the outer world. When we give form to the feelings we experience, so that they enlighten us concerning the outer world, our thoughts, judgments and feelings become knowledge of the outer world. Through the Consciousness Soul we explore the secrets of the outer world as human beings endowed with knowledge and cognition.

So does the Ego work continually in the Sentient Soul, in the Intellectual or Mind-Soul, and in the Consciousness Soul, releasing the forces inwardly bound up there and enabling man to advance in his evolution by enriching his capacities. The Ego is the actor, the active being through whose agency man himself takes control of his evolution and progresses from life to life, remedying the defects of former lives and widening the faculties of his soul. Such is human evolution from life to life; it consists first of all in the Ego's work on the soul in its threefold aspect.

We must, however, recognise clearly that in its work the Ego has the character of a "two-edged sword". Yes, this human Ego is, on the one hand, the element in man's being through which alone he can be truly man. If we lacked this central point, we should be merged passively with the outer world. Our concepts and ideas have to be taken hold of in this centre; more and more of them must be experienced; and our inner life must be increasingly enriched by impressions from the outer world. Man is truly man to the degree in which his Ego becomes richer and more comprehensive. Hence the Ego must seek to enrich itself in the course of succeeding lives; it must become a centre whereby man is not simply part of the outer world but acts as a stimulating force upon it. The richer the fund of his impulses, the more he has absorbed and the more he radiates from the centre of his individual self, the nearer he approaches to being truly man.

That is one aspect of the Ego; and we are in duty bound to endeavour to make the Ego as rich and as many-sided as we can. But the reverse side of this progress is manifest in what we call selfishness or egoism. If these words were taken as catchwords and it were said that human beings must become selfless, that of course would be bad, as any use of catchwords always is. It is indeed man's task to enrich himself inwardly, but this does not imply a selfish hardening of the Ego and a shutting off of itself with its riches from the world. In that event a man would indeed become richer and richer, but he would lose his connection with the world. His enrichment would signify that the world had no more to give him, nor he the world. In the course of time he would perish, for while striving to enrich his Ego he would keep it all for himself and would become isolated from the world. This caricature of development would impoverish a man's Ego to an increasing extent, for selfishness

The Mission of Anger

lays a man inwardly waste. So is it that the Ego, as it works in the three members of the soul, acts as a two-edged sword. On the one hand, it must work to become always richer, a powerful centre from which much can stream forth; but on the other hand it must bring everything it absorbs back into harmony with the outer world. To the same degree that it develops its own resources, it must go out from itself and relate itself to the whole of existence. It must become simultaneously an independent being and a selfless one. Only when the Ego works in these two apparently contradictory directions—when on one side it enriches itself increasingly and on the other side becomes selfless—can human evolution go forward so as to be satisfying for man and health-giving for the whole of existence. The Ego has to work on each of three soul-members in such a way that both sides of human development are kept in balance.

Now the work of the Ego in the soul leads to its own gradual awakening. Development occurs in all forms of life, and we find that the three members of the human soul are today at very different stages of evolution. The Sentient Soul, the bearer of our emotions and impulses and of all the feelings that are aroused by direct stimuli from the outer world, is the most strongly developed of the three. But at certain lower stages of evolution the content of the Sentient Soul is experienced in a dull, dim way, for the Ego is not yet fully awake. When a man works inwardly on himself and his soul-life progresses, the Ego becomes more and more clearly conscious of itself. But as far as the Sentient Soul is awake, the Ego is hardly more than a brooding presence within it. The Ego gains in clarity when man advances to a richer life in the Intellectual Soul, and achieves full clarity in the Consciousness Soul. Man then comes to be aware of himself as an individual who stands apart from his environment and is active in gaining objective knowledge of it. This is possible only when the Ego is awake in the Consciousness Soul.

Thus we have the Ego only dimly awake in the Sentient Soul. It is swept along by waves of pleasure and pain, joy and sorrow, and can scarcely be perceived as an entity. In the Intellectual Soul, when clearly defined ideas and judgments are developed, the Ego first gains clarity, and achieves full clarity in the Consciousness Soul.

Hence we can say: Man has a duty to educate himself through his Ego and so to further his own inner progress. But at the time of its awakening the Ego is still given over to the waves of emotion that surge through the Sentient Soul. Is there anything in the Sentient Soul which can contribute to the education of the Ego at a time when the Ego is still incapable of educating itself?

We shall see how in the Intellectual Soul there is something which enables the Ego to take its own education in hand. In the Sentient Soul this is not yet possible; the Ego must be guided by something which arises independently within the Sentient Soul. We will single out this one element in the Sentient Soul and consider its two-sided mission for educating the Ego. This element is one to which the strongest objection may perhaps be taken—the emotion we call anger. Anger arises in the Sentient Soul when the Ego is still dormant there. Or can it be said that we stand in a self-conscious relation to anyone if their behaviour causes us to flare up in anger?

Let us picture the difference between two persons: two teachers, let us say. One of them has achieved the clarity which makes for enlightened inner judgments. He sees what his pupil is doing wrong but is not perturbed by it, because his Intellectual Soul is mature. With his Consciousness Soul, also, he is calmly aware of the child's error, and if necessary he can prescribe an appropriate penalty, not impelled by any emotional reaction but in accordance with ethical and pedagogical judgment. It will be otherwise with a teacher whose Ego has not reached the stage that would enable him to remain calm and discerning. Not knowing what to do, he flares up in anger at the child's misdemeanour.

Is such anger always inappropriate to the event that calls it forth? No, not always. And this is something we must keep in mind. Before we are capable of judging an event in the light of the Intellectual Soul or the Consciousness Soul, the wisdom of evolution has provided for us to be overcome by emotion because of that event. Something in our Sentient Soul is activated by an event in the outer world. We are not yet capable of making the right response as an act of judgment, but we can react from the emotional centre of the Sentient Soul. Of all things that the Sentient Soul experiences, let us therefore consider anger.

It points to what will come about in the future. To begin with, anger expresses a judgment of some event in the outer world; then, having learnt unconsciously through anger to react to something wrong, we advance gradually to enlightened judgments in our higher souls. So in certain respects anger is an educator. It arises in us as an inner experience before we are mature enough to form an enlightened judgment of right and wrong. This is how we should look on the anger which can flare up in a young man, before he is capable of a considered judgment, at the sight of injustice or folly which violates his ideals; and then we can properly speak of a righteous anger. No-one does better at acquiring an inner capacity for sound judgment than a man who has started from a state of soul in which he could be moved to righteous anger by anything ignoble, immoral or crazy. That is how anger has the mission of raising

The Mission of Anger

the Ego to higher levels. On the other hand, since man is to become a free being, everything human can degenerate. Anger can degenerate into rage and serve to gratify the worst kind of egoism. This must be so, if man is to advance towards freedom. But we must not fail to realise that the very thing which can lapse into evil may, when it manifests in its true significance, have the mission of furthering the progress of man. It is because man can change good into evil, that good qualities, when they are developed in the right way, can become a possession of the Ego. So is anger to be understood as the harbinger of that which can raise man to calm self-possession.

But although anger is on the one hand an educator of the Ego, it also serves strangely enough, to engender selflessness. What is the Ego's response when anger overcomes it at the sight of injustice or folly? Something within us speaks out against the spectacle confronting us. Our anger illustrates the fact that we are up against something in the outer world. The Ego then makes its presence felt and seeks to safeguard itself against this outer event. The whole content of the Ego is involved. If the sight of injustice or folly were not to kindle a noble anger in us, the events in the outer world would carry us along with them as an easy-going spectator; we would not feel the sting of the Ego and we would have no concern for its development. Anger enriches the Ego and summons it to confront the outer world, yet at the same time it induces selflessness. For if anger is such that it can be called noble and does not lapse into blind rage, its effect is to damp down Ego-feeling and to produce something like powerlessness in the soul. If the soul is suffused with anger, its own activity becomes increasingly suppressed.

This experience of anger is wonderfully well brought out in the vernacular use of *sich giften,* to poison oneself, as a phrase meaning "to get angry". This is an example of how popular imagination arrives at a truth which may often elude the learned.

Anger which eats into the soul is a poison; it damps down the Ego's self-awareness and so promotes selflessness. Thus we see how anger serves to teach both independence and selflessness; that is its dual mission as an educator of humanity, before the Ego is ripe to undertake its own education. If we were not enabled by anger to take an independent stand in cases where the outer world offends our inner feeling, we would not be selfless, but dependent and Ego-less in the worst sense.

For the spiritual scientist, anger is also the harbinger of something quite different. Life shows us that a person who is unable to flare up with anger at injustice or folly will never develop true kindness and love. Equally, a person who educates himself through noble anger will have a heart abounding in love, and through love he will do good. Love and kindness are the obverse of noble anger. Anger that is overcome and purified will be transformed into the love that is its counterpart. A loving hand is seldom one that has never been clenched in response to injustice or folly. Anger and love are complementary.

A superficial Theosophy might say: Yes, a man must overcome his passions; he must cleanse and purify them. But overcoming something does not mean shirking or shunning it. It is a strange sort of sacrifice that is made by someone who proposes to cast off his passionate self by evading it. We cannot sacrifice something unless we have first possessed it. Anger can be overcome only by someone who has experienced it first within himself. Instead of trying to evade such emotions, we must transmute them in ourselves. By transmuting anger, we rise from the Sentient Soul, where noble anger can flame out, to the Intellectual Soul and the Consciousness Soul, where love and the power to give blessing are born.

Transmuted anger is love in action. That is what we learn from reality. Anger in moderation has the mission of leading human beings to love; we can call it the teacher of love. And not in vain do we call the undefined power that flows from the wisdom of the world and shows itself in the righting of wrongs the "wrath of God", in contrast to God's love. But we know that these two things belong together; without the other, neither can exist. In life they require and determine each other.

Now let us see how in art and poetry, when they are great, the primal wisdom of the world is revealed.

When we come to speak of the mission of truth, we shall see how Goethe's thoughts on this subject are clearly expressed in his *Pandora,* one of his finest poems, though small in scale. And in a powerful poem of universal significance, the *Prometheus Bound* by Aeschylus, we are brought to see, though perhaps less clearly, the role of anger as a phenomenon in world history.

Probably you know the legend on which Aeschylus based his drama. Prometheus is a descendant of the ancient race of Titans, who had succeeded the first generation of gods in the evolution of the earth and of humanity. Ouranos and Gaia belong to the first generation of gods. Ouranus is succeeded by Kronos (Saturn). Then the Titans are overthrown by the third generation of gods, led by Zeus. Prometheus, though a descendant of the Titans, was on the side of Zeus in the battle against the Titans and so could be called a friend of Zeus, but he was only half a friend. When Zeus took over the rulership of the earth—so the legend continues—humanity had advanced far enough to enter on a new phase, while the old faculties possessed by men in ancient times

The Mission of Anger

were dying out. Zeus wanted to exterminate mankind and instal a new race on earth, but Prometheus resolved to give men the means of further progress. He brought them speech and writing, knowledge of the outer world, and, finally, fire, in order that by learning to master these tools humanity might raise itself from the low level to which it had sunk.

If we look more deeply into the story, we find that everything bestowed by Prometheus on mankind is connected with the human Ego, while Zeus is portrayed as a divine power which inspires and ensouls men in whom the Ego has not yet come to full expression. If we look back over the evolution of the earth, we find in the far past a humanity in which the Ego was no more than an obscurely brooding presence. It had to acquire certain definite faculties with which to educate itself. The gifts that Zeus could bestow were not adapted to furthering the progress of mankind. In respect of the astral body, and of everything in man apart from his Ego, Zeus is the giver. Because Zeus was not capable of promoting the development of the Ego, he resolved to wipe out mankind. All the gifts brought by Prometheus, on the other hand, enabled the Ego to educate itself. Such is the deeper meaning of the legend.

Prometheus, accordingly, is the one who enables the Ego to set to work on enriching and enlarging itself; and that is exactly how the gifts bestowed by Prometheus were understood in ancient Greece.

Now we have seen, that if the Ego concentrates on this single aim, it finally impoverishes itself, for it will be shutting itself off from the outer world. Enriching itself is one side only of the Ego's task. It has to go out and bring its inner wealth into harmony with the world around it, if it is not to be impoverished in the long run. Prometheus could bestow on men only the gifts whereby the Ego could enrich itself. Thus, inevitably, he challenged the powers which act from out of the entire cosmos to subdue the Ego in the right way, so that it may become selfless and thus develop its other aspect. The independence of the Ego, achieved under the sting of anger on the one hand, and on the other the damping down of the Ego when a man consumes his anger, as it were, and his Ego is deadened—this whole process is presented in the historic pictures of the conflict between Prometheus and Zeus.

Prometheus endows the Ego with faculties which enable it to become richer and richer. What Zeus has to do is to produce the same effect that anger has in the individual. Thus the wrath of Zeus falls on Prometheus and extinguishes the power of the Ego in him. The legend tells us how Prometheus is punished by Zeus for the untimely stimulus he had given to the advancement of the human Ego. He is chained to a rock.

Metamorphoses of the Soul

The suffering thus endured by the human Ego and its inner rebellion are magnificently expressed by Aeschylus in this poetic drama. So we see the representative of the human Ego subdued by the wrath of Zeus. Just as the individual human Ego is checked and driven back on itself when it has to swallow its anger, so is Prometheus chained by the wrath of Zeus, meaning that his activity is reduced to its proper level. When a flood of anger sweeps through the soul of an individual, his Ego, striving for self-expression, finds itself enchained; so was the Promethean Ego chained to a rock.

That is the peculiar merit of this legend: it presents in powerful pictures far-reaching truths which are valid both for individuals and for humanity at large. People could see in these pictures what had to be experienced in the individual soul. Thus in Prometheus chained to the Caucasian rock we can see a representative of the human Ego at a time when the Ego, striving to advance from its brooding somnolence in the Sentient Soul, is restrained by its fetters from indulging in wild extravagance.

We are then told how Prometheus knows that the wrath of Zeus will be silenced when he is overthrown by the son of a mortal. He will be succeeded in his rulership by someone born of mortal man. The Ego is released by the mission of anger on a lower plane, and the immortal Ego, the immortal human soul, will be born from mortal man on a higher plane. Prometheus looks forward to the time when Zeus will be succeeded by Christ Jesus, and the individual Ego will itself be transformed into the loving Ego when the noble anger that fettered it is transformed into love. We behold the birth from the Ego enchained by anger of that other Ego, whose action in the outer world will be that of love and blessing. So, too, we behold the birth of a God of love who tends and cherishes the Ego; the very Ego that in earlier times was fettered by the anger of Zeus, so that it should not transgress its proper bounds.

Hence we see in the continuation of this legend an external picture of human evolution. We must ourselves take hold of this myth in such a way that it gives us a living picture, universally relevant, of how the individual experiences the transformation of the Ego, educated by the mission of anger, into the liberated Ego imbued with love. Then we understand what the legend does and what Aeschylus made of his material. We feel the soul's life-blood pulsing through us; we feel it in the continuation of the legend and in the dramatic form given to it by Aeschylus. So we find in this Greek drama something like a practical application of processes we can experience in our own souls. This is true of all great poems and other works of art: they spring from typical

The Mission of Anger

great experiences of the human soul.

We have seen today how the Ego is educated through the purification of a passion. In the next lecture we shall see how the Ego becomes ripe to educate itself in the Intellectual Soul by learning to grasp the mission of truth on a higher plane. We have seen also how in our considerations today the saying of Heraclitus is borne out: "You will never find the boundaries of the soul, by whatever paths you search for them; so wide and deep is the being of the soul."

Yes, it is true that the soul's being is so far-reaching that we cannot directly sound its depths. But Spiritual Science, with the opened eye of the seer, leads into the substance of the soul, and we can progress further and further into fathoming the mysterious being that the human soul is when we contemplate it through the eyes of the spiritual scientist. On the one hand we can truly say: The soul has unfathomable depths, but if we take this saying in full earnest we can add: The boundaries of the soul are indeed so wide that we have to search for them by all possible paths, but we can hope that by extending these boundaries ourselves, we shall progress further and further in our knowledge of the soul.

This ray of hope will illumine our search for knowledge if we accept the true words of Heraclitus not with resignation but with confidence: The boundaries of the soul are so wide that you may search along every path and not reach them, so comprehensive is the being of the soul.

Let us try to grasp this comprehensive being; it will lead us on further and further towards a solution of the riddles of existence.

LECTURE 3
The Mission of Truth

Berlin, 22nd October, 1909

We were able to close our lecture on the Mission of Anger (illustrated in *Prometheus Bound*) with the saying of Heraclitus: "Never will you find the boundaries of the soul, by whatever paths you search for them; so all-embracing is the soul's being." We came to know this depth in the working and interplay of the powers of the soul; and the truth of the saying came home to us especially when we turned our attention to the most deeply inward part of man's being. Man is most spiritual in his Ego, and that was our starting-point.

The Ego complements those other elements of man's being which he has in common with minerals, plants and animals. He has his physical body in common with minerals, plants and animals; his etheric body in common with animals and plants; his astral body in common with animals. Through his Ego he first becomes man in the true sense and is able to progress from stage to stage. It is the Ego that works upon the other members of his being; it cleanses and purifies the instincts, inclinations, desires and passions of the astral body, and will lead the etheric and physical bodies on to ever-higher stages. But if we look at the Ego, we find that this high member of man's being is imprisoned, as it were, between two extremes.

Through his Ego, man is intended to become increasingly a being who has a firm centre in himself. His thoughts, feelings and will-impulses should spring from this centre. The more he has a firm and well-endowed centre in himself, the more will he have to give to the world; the stronger and richer will be his activities and everything that goes out from him. If he is unable to find this central point in himself, he will be in danger of losing himself through a misconceived activity of his Ego. He would lose himself in the world and go ineffectually through life. Or he may lapse into the other extreme. Just as he may lose himself if he fails to strengthen and enrich his Ego, so, if he thinks of nothing

The Mission of Truth

but developing his Ego, he may fall into the other extreme of selfish isolation from all human community. Here, on this other side, we find egoism, with its hardening and secluding influence, which can divert the Ego from its proper path. The Ego is confined within these two extremes.

In considering the human soul, we called three of its members the Sentient Soul, the Intellectual Soul and the Consciousness Soul. We also came to recognise—surprisingly, perhaps, for many people—that anger acts as a kind of educator of the Sentient Soul. A one-sided view of the lecture on the mission of anger could give scope for many objections. But if we go into the underlying significance of this view of anger, we shall find in it an answer to many important riddles of life.

In what sense is anger an educator of the soul—especially the Sentient Soul—and a forerunner of love? Is it not true that anger tends to make a man lose control of himself and engage in wild, immoral and loveless behaviour? If we are thinking only of wild, unjustified outbursts of anger, we shall get a false idea of what the mission of anger is. It is not through unjustified outbreaks of anger that anger educates the soul, but through its inward action on the soul.

Let us again imagine two teachers faced with children who have done something wrong. One teacher will burst into anger and hastily impose a penalty. The other teacher, though unable to break out into anger, is also incapable of acting rightly, with perfect tranquillity, out of his Ego, in the sense described yesterday. How will the behaviour of two such teachers differ? An outburst of anger by one of them involves more than the penalty imposed on the child. Anger agitates the soul and works upon it in such a way as to destroy selfishness. Anger acts like a poison on selfishness, and we find that in time it gradually transforms the powers of the soul and makes it capable of love. On the other hand, if a teacher has not yet attained inner tranquillity and yet inflicts a coldly calculated penalty, he will—since anger will not work in him as a counteracting poison—become increasingly a cold egoist.

Anger works inwardly and can be regarded as a regulator for unjustified outbursts of selfishness. Anger must be there or it could not be fought against. In overcoming anger the soul continually improves itself. If a man insists on getting something done that he considers right and loses his temper over it, his anger will dampen the egoistic forces in his soul; it reduces their effective power. Just because anger is overcome and a man frees himself from it and rises above it, his selflessness will be enhanced and the selflessness of his Ego continually strengthened. The scene of this interplay between anger and the Ego is the Sentient Soul. A different interplay between the soul and other experiences takes its course in the Intellectual Soul.

Although the soul has attributes which it must overcome in order to rise above them, it must also develop inwardly certain forces which it should love and cherish, however spontaneously they may arise. They are forces to which the soul may initially yield, so that, when it finally asserts itself, it is not weakened, but strengthened, by the experience. If a man were incapable of anger when called upon to assert himself in action, he would be the weaker for it.

It is just when a man lovingly immerses himself in his own soul that his soul is strengthened and an ascent to higher stages of the Ego comes within reach. The outstanding element that the soul may love within itself, leading not to egoism but to selflessness, is truth. Truth educates the Intellectual Soul. While anger is an attribute of the soul that must be overcome if a man is to rise to higher stages, truth should be loved and valued from the start. An inward cultivation of truth is essential for the progress of the soul.

How is it that devotion to truth leads man upwards from stage to stage? The opposites of truth are falsehood and error. We shall see how man progresses in so far as he overcomes falsehood and error and pursues truth as his great ideal.

A higher truth must be the aim of man's endeavour, while he treats anger as an enemy to be increasingly abolished. He must love truth and feel himself most intimately united with it. Nevertheless, eminent poets and thinkers have rightly claimed that full possession of truth is beyond human reach. Lessing,[21] for example, says that pure truth is not for men, but only a perpetual striving towards it. He speaks of truth as a distant goddess whom men may approach but never reach. When the nature of truth stirs the soul to strive for it, the soul can be impelled to rise from stage to stage. Since there is this everlasting search for truth, and since truth is so manifold in meaning, all we can reasonably say is that man must set out to grasp truth and to kindle in himself a genuine sense of truth. Hence we cannot speak of a single, all-embracing truth.

In this lecture we will consider the idea of truth in its right sense, and it will become clear that by cultivating a sense of truth in his inner life man will be imbued with a progressive power that leads him to selflessness.

Man strives towards truth; but when people try to form views concerning one thing or another, we find that in the most varied realms of life conflicting opinions are advanced. When we see what different people take for truth, we might think that the striving for truth leads inevitably to the most contradictory views and standpoints. However, if we look impartially at the facts, we shall find guidelines which show

The Mission of Truth

how it is that men who are all seeking truth, arrive at such a diversity of opinions.

Let us take an example. The American multimillionaire, Harriman,[22] who died recently, was a rarity among millionaires in concerning himself with thoughts of general human interest. His aphorisms, found after his death, include a remarkable statement. He wrote: No man in this world is indispensable. When one goes, another is there to take his place. When I lay down my work, another will come and take it up. The railways will continue running, dividends will be paid; and so, strictly speaking, it is with all men.

This millionaire, accordingly, rose to the point of declaring as a generally valid truth—no man is indispensable!

Let us compare this statement with a remark by a man who worked for many years in Berlin and gained great distinction through his lecture-courses on the lives of Michelangelo, Raphael and Goethe—I mean the art-historian Herman Grimm.[23] When Treitschke[24] died, Herman Grimm wrote of him roughly as follows: Now Treitschke is gone, and people only now realise what he accomplished. No-one can take his place and continue his work in the same way. A feeling prevails that in the circle where he taught, everything is changed. Note that Herman Grimm did not add the words, so it is with all men.

Here we have two men, the American millionaire and Herman Grimm, who arrive at exactly opposite truths. How does this come about? If we carefully compare the two statements, we shall find a clue. Bear in mind that Harriman says pointedly: When I lay down my work, someone else will continue it. He does not get away from himself. The other thinker, Herman Grimm, leaves himself entirely out of account. He does not speak about himself, or ask what sort of opinions or truths others might gain from him. He merges himself in his subject. Anyone with a feeling for the matter will have no doubt as to which of the two spoke truth. We need only ask—who carried on Goethe's work when he laid it down? We can feel that Harriman's reflections suffer from the fact that he fails to get away from himself. Up to a point we may conclude that it is prejudicial to truth if someone in search of truth cannot get away from himself. Truth is best served when the seeker leaves himself out of the reckoning. Would it be true to say, then, that truth is already something that gives us a view (*Ansicht*) of things?

A view, in the sense of an opinion, is a thought which reflects the outer world. When we form a thought or reach a decision about something, does it follow that we have a *true* picture of it?

Suppose you take a photograph of a remarkable tree. Does the

35

photograph give a true picture of the tree? It shows the tree from one side only, not the whole reality of the tree. No-one could form a true image of the tree from this one photograph. How could anyone who has not seen the tree be brought nearer to the truth of it? If the tree were photographed from four sides, he could collate the photographs and arrive finally at a true picture of the tree, not dependent on a particular standpoint.

Now let us apply this example to human beings. A man who leaves himself out of account when forming a view of something is doing much the same as the photographer who goes all round the tree. He eliminates himself by conscious action. When we form an opinion or take a certain view, we must realise that all such opinions depend on our personal standpoint, our habits of mind and our individuality. If we then try to eliminate these influences from our search for truth, we shall be acting as the photographer did in our example. The first condition for acquiring a genuine sense of truth is that we should get away from ourselves and see clearly how much depends on our personal point of view. If the American multimillionaire had got away from himself he would have known that there was a difference between him and other men.

An example from everyday life has shown us, that if a man fails to realise how much his personal standpoint or point of departure influences his views, he will arrive at narrow opinions, not at the truth. This is apparent also on a wider scale. Anyone who looks at the true spiritual evolution of mankind, and compares all the various "truths" that have arisen in the course of time, will find—if he looks deeply enough—that when people pronounce a "truth" they ought first of all to get away from their individual outlooks. It will then become clear that the most varied opinions concerning truth are advanced because men have not recognised to what extent their views are restricted by their personal standpoints.

A less familiar example may lead to a deeper understanding of this matter. If we want to learn more about beauty, we turn to aesthetics, which deals with the forms of beauty. Beauty is something we encounter in the outer world. How can we learn the truth about it? Here again we must free ourselves from the restrictions imposed by our personal characteristics.

Take for example the 19th century German thinker, Solger.[25] He wished to investigate the nature of beauty in accordance with his idea of truth. He could not deny that we meet with beauty in the external world; but he was a man with a one-sided theosophical outlook, and this was reflected in his theory of aesthetics. His interest in a beautiful

The Mission of Truth

picture was confined to the shining through it of the only kind of spirituality he recognised. For him, an object was beautiful only in so far as the spiritual was manifest through it. Solger was a one-sided theosophist; he sought to explain sense-perceptible phenomena in terms of the supersensible; but he forgot that sense-perceptible reality has a justified existence on its own account. Unable to escape from his preconceptions, he sought to attain to the spiritual by way of a misconceived theosophy.

Another writer on aesthetics, Robert Zimmermann,[26] came to an exactly opposite conclusion. As against Solger's misconceived theosophical aesthetics, Zimmermann based his aesthetics on a misconceived anti-theosophical outlook. His sole concern was with symmetry and anti-symmetry, harmony and discord. He had no interest in going beyond the beautiful to that which manifests through it. So his aesthetics were as one-sided as Soger's. Every striving for truth can be vitiated if the seeker fails to recognise that he must first endeavour to get away from himself. This can be achieved only gradually; but the primary, inexorable demand is, that if we are to advance towards truth we must leave ourselves out of account and quite forget ourselves. Truth has a unique characteristic: a man can strive for it while remaining entirely within himself and yet—while living in his Ego—he can acquire something which, fundamentally speaking, has nothing to do with the egoistic ego.

Whenever a man tries in life to get his own way in some matter, this is an expression of his egoism. Whenever he wants to force on others something he thinks right and loses his temper over it, that is an expression of his self-seeking. This self-seeking must be subdued before he can attain to truth. Truth is something we experience in our most inward being—and yet it liberates us increasingly from ourselves. Of course, it is essential that nothing save the love of truth should enter into our striving for it. If passions, instincts and desires, from which the Sentient Soul must be cleansed before the Intellectual Soul can strive for truth, come into it, they will prevent a man from getting away from himself and will keep his Ego tied to a fixed viewpoint. In the search for truth, the only passion that must not be discarded is love.

Truth is a lofty goal. This is shown by the fact that truth, in the sense intended here, is recognised today in one limited realm only. It is only in the realm of mathematics that humanity in general has reached the goal of truth, for here men have curbed their passions and desires and kept them out of the way. Why are all men agreed that three times three makes nine and not ten? Because no emotion comes into it. Men would agree on the highest truths if they had gone as far with them as they have with mathematics. The truths of mathematics are grasped in the inmost soul, and because they are grasped in this way, we possess them. We would still possess them if a hundred or a thousand people were to contradict us; we would still know that three times three makes nine because we have grasped this fact inwardly. If the hundred or thousand people who take a different view were to get away from themselves, they would come to the same truth.

What, then, is the way to mutual understanding and unity for mankind? We understand one another in the field of reckoning and counting because here we have met the conditions required. Peace, concord and harmony will prevail among men to the extent that they find truth. That is the essential thing: that we should seek for truth as something to be found only in our own deepest being; and should know that truth ever and again draws men together, because from the innermost depth of every human soul its light shines forth.

So is truth the leader of mankind towards unity and mutual understanding, and also the precursor of justice and love. Truth is a precursor we must cherish, while the other precursor, anger, that we came to know yesterday, must be overcome if we are to be led by it away from selfishness. That is the mission of truth: to become the object of increasing love and care and devotion on our part. Inasmuch as we devote ourselves inwardly to truth, our true self gains in strength and will enable us to cast off self-interest. Anger weakens us; truth strengthens us.

Truth is a stern goddess; she demands to be at the centre of a unique love in our souls. If man fails to get away from himself and his desires and prefers something else to her, she takes immediate revenge. The English poet Coleridge has rightly indicated how a man should stand towards truth. If, he says, a man loves Christianity more than truth, he will soon find that he loves his own Christian sect more than Christianity, and then he will find that he loves himself more than his sect.

Very much is implicit in these words. Above all, they signify that to strive against truth leads to humanly degrading egoism. Love of truth is the only love that sets the Ego free. And directly man gives priority to anything else, he falls inevitably into self-seeking. Herein lies the great and most serious importance of truth for the education of the human soul. Truth conforms to no man, and only by devotion to truth can truth be found. Directly man prefers himself and his own opinions to the truth, he becomes anti-social and alienates himself from the human community. Look at people who make no attempt to love truth for its own sake but parade their own opinions as the truth: they care for nothing but the content of their own souls and are the most intolerant. Those who love truth in terms of their own views and

The Mission of Truth

opinions will not suffer anyone to reach truth along a quite different path. They put every obstacle in the way of anyone with different abilities, who comes to opinions unlike their own. Hence the conflicts that so often arise in life. An honest striving for truth leads to human understanding, but the love of truth for the sake of one's own personality leads to intolerance and the destruction of other people's freedom.

Truth is experienced in the Intellectual Soul. It can be sought for and attained through personal effort only by beings capable of thought. Inasmuch as truth is acquired by thinking, we must realise very clearly that there are two kinds of truth. First we have the truth that comes from observing the world of Nature around us and investigating it bit by bit in order to discover its truths, laws and wisdom. When we contemplate the whole range of our experience of the world in this way, we come to the kind of truth that can be called the truth derived from "reflective" thinking—we first observe the world and then think about our findings.

We saw yesterday that the entire realm of Nature is permeated with wisdom, and that wisdom lives in all natural things. In a plant there lives the idea of the plant, and this we can arrive at by reflective thought. Similarly, we can discern the wisdom that lives in the plant. By thus looking out on the world we can infer that the world is born of wisdom, and that through the activity of our thinking we can rediscover the element that enters into the creation of the world. That is the kind of truth to be gained by reflective thought.

There are also other truths. These cannot be gained by reflective thought, but only by going beyond everything that can be learnt from the outer world. In ordinary life we can see at once that when a man constructs a tool or some other instrument, he has to formulate laws that are not part of the outer world. For example, no-one could learn from the outer world how to construct a clock, for the laws of Nature are not so arranged as to provide for the appearance of clocks as a natural product. That is a second kind of truth: we come to it by thinking out something not given to us by observation or experience of the outer world. Hence there are these two kinds of truth, and they must be kept strictly apart, one derived from reflective thought and the other from "creative" thought.

How can a truth of this second kind be verified? The inventor of a clock can easily prove that he had thought it out correctly. He has to show that the clock does what he expects. Anything we think out in advance must prove itself in practice: it must yield results that can be recognised in the external world. The truths of Spiritual Science or Anthroposophy are of this kind. They cannot be found by observing external experience.

For example, no findings in the realm of outer Nature can establish the truth we have often dwelt on in connection with the immortal kernel of man's being: the truth that the human Ego appears again and again on earth in successive incarnations. Anyone who wishes to acquire this truth must raise himself above ordinary experience. He must grasp in his soul a truth that has then to be made real in outer life. A truth of this kind cannot be proved in the same way as truths of the first kind, gained by what we have called reflective thought. It can be proven only by showing how it applies to life and is reflected there. If we look at life with the knowledge that the soul repeatedly returns and ever and again goes through a series of events and experiences between birth and death, we shall find how much satisfaction, how much strength and fruitfulness, these thoughts can bring. Or again, if we ask how the soul of a child can be helped to develop and grow stronger, if we presuppose that an eternally existent soul is here working its way into a new life, then this truth will shine in on us and give proof of its fruitfulness in daily experience. Any other proofs are false. The only way in which a truth of this kind can be confirmed is by giving proof of its validity in daily life. Hence there is a vast difference between these two kinds of truth. Those of the second kind are grasped in the spirit and then verified by observing their influence on outer life.

What then is the educational effect of these two kinds of truth on the human soul? It makes a great difference whether a man devotes himself to truths that come from reflective thought or to those that come from creative thought. If we steep ourselves in the wisdom of Nature and create in ourselves a true reflection of it, we can rightly say that we have in ourselves something of the creative activity from which the life of Nature springs. But here a distinction must be made. The wisdom of Nature is directly creative and gives rise to the reality of Nature in all its fullness, but the truth we derive from thinking about Nature is only a passive image; in our thinking it has lost its power. We may indeed acquire a wide, open-minded picture of natural truth, but the creative, productive element is absent from it. Hence the immediate effect of this picture of truth on the development of the human Ego is desolating. The creative power of the Ego is crippled and devitalised; the Self loses strength and can no longer stand up to the world, if it is concerned only with reflective thoughts. Nothing else does so much to isolate the Ego, to make it withdraw into itself and look with hostility on the world. A man can become a cold egoist if he is intent only on investigating the outer world. Why does he want this knowledge? Does he mean to place it at the service of the Gods?

The Mission of Truth

If a man desires only this kind of truth, he wants it for himself, and he will be on the way to becoming a cold egoist and misogynist in later life. He will become a recluse or will sever himself from mankind in some other way, for he wants to possess the content of the world as his own truth. All forms of seclusion and hostility towards humanity can be found on this path. The soul becomes increasingly dried up and loses its sense of human fellowship. It becomes ever more impoverished, although the truth should enrich it. Whether a man turns into a recluse or a one-sided eccentric makes no difference; in both cases a hardening process will overtake his soul. Hence we see that the more a man confines himself to this kind of reflective thought, the less fruitful his soul will be. Let us try to understand why this is so.

Consider the realms of nature and suppose that we have before us an array of plants. They have been formed by the living wisdom which calls forth their inherent productive power. Now an artist comes along. His soul receives the picture that Nature sets before him. He does not merely think about it; he opens himself to Nature's productive power and lets it work upon him. He creates a work of art which does not embody merely an act of thinking; it is imbued with productive power. Then comes someone who tries to get behind the picture and to extract a thought from it. He ponders over it. In this way its reality is filtered and impoverished. Now try to carry this process further. Once the soul has extracted a thought from the picture, it has finished with it. Nothing more can be done except to formulate thoughts about the thought—an absurd procedure which soon dries up.

It is quite different with creative thinking. Here a man is himself productive. His thoughts take form as realities in outer life; here he is working after the example of Nature herself. That is how it is with a man who goes beyond mere observation and reflective thinking and allows something not to be gained from observation to arise in his soul. All spiritual-scientific truths require a productive disposition in the soul. In the case of these truths all mere reflective thinking is bad and leads to deception. But the truths attainable by creative thought are limited, for man is weak in the face of the creative wisdom of the world. There is no end to the things from which we can derive truths by reflective thought; but creative thought, although the field open to it is restricted, brings about a heightening of productive power; the soul is refreshed and its scope extended. Indeed, the soul becomes more and more inwardly divine, in so far as it reflects in itself an essential element of the divine creative activity in the world.

So we have these two distinct kinds of truth, one reached by creative thought, the other by reflective thought. This latter kind, derived from the investigation of existent things or current experience, will always lead to abstractions; under its influence the soul is deprived of nourishment and tends to dry up. The truth that is not gained from immediate experience is creative; its strength helps man to find a place in the world where he can co-operate in shaping the future.

The past can be approached only by reflective thought, while creative thought opens a way into the future. Man thus becomes a responsible creator of the future. He extends the power of his Ego into the future, in so far as he comes to possess not merely the truths derived from the past by reflective thinking, but also those that are gained by creative thinking and point towards the future.

Herein lies the liberating influence of creative thinking. Anyone who is active in the striving for truth will soon find how he is impoverished by mere reflective thinking. He will come to understand how the devotee of reflective thinking fills his mind with phantom ideas and bloodless abstractions. Such a man may feel like an outcast, condemned to a mere savouring of truth and may come to doubt whether his spirit can play any part in shaping the world. On the other hand, a man who experiences a truth gained by creative thinking will find that it nourishes and warms his soul and gives it new strength for every stage in life. It fills him with joy when he is able to grasp truths of this kind and discovers that in bringing them to bear on the phenomena of life he can say to himself: Now I not only understand what is going on there, but I can explain it in the light of having known something of it previously.

With the aid of spiritual-scientific truths we can now approach man himself. He cannot be understood merely by reflective thinking, but now we can comprehend him better and better, while our feeling of unity with the world and our interest in it are continually enhanced. We experience joy and satisfaction at every confirmation of spiritual-scientific truths that we encounter. This is what makes these truths so satisfying: we have first to grasp them before we can find them corroborated in actual life, and all the while they enrich us inwardly. We are drawn gradually into unity with the phenomena we experience. We get away more and more from ourselves, whereas reflective thinking leads to subtle forms of egoism. In order to find confirmation of truths gained by creative thinking we have to go out from ourselves and look for their application in all realms of life. It is these truths that liberate us from ourselves and imbue us in the highest degree with a sense of truth and a feeling for it.

Feelings of this kind have been alive in every genuine seeker after truth. They were deeply present in the soul of Goethe when he declared:

The Mission of Truth

"Only that which is fruitful is true"—a magnificent, luminous saying of far-reaching import. But Goethe was also well aware that men must be closely united with truth if they are to understand one another. Nothing does more to estrange men from one another than a lack of concern for truth and the search for truth. Goethe also said: "A false doctrine cannot be refuted, for it rests on a conviction that the false is true."[27] Obviously there are falsities that can be logically disproved, but that is not what Goethe means. He is convinced that a false viewpoint cannot be refuted by logical conclusions, and that the fruitful application of truth in practical life should be our sole guide-line in our search for truth.

It was because Goethe was so wonderfully united with truth that he was able to sketch the beautiful poetic drama, *Pandora,* which he began to write in 1807. Though only a fragment, *Pandora* is a ripe product of his creative genius—so powerful in every line, that anyone who responds to it must feel it to be an example of the purest, grandest art. We see in it how Goethe was able to make a start towards the greatest truths—but then lacked the strength to go further. The task was too arduous for him to carry through; but we have enough of it to get some idea of how deeply he had penetrated into the problems of spiritual education. He had a clear vision of everything that the soul has to overcome in order to rise higher; he understood everything we learnt yesterday about anger and the fettered Prometheus, and have learnt today about that other educator of the soul, the sense of truth.

How closely related these two things are in their effects on the soul can be seen also in the facial expressions they call forth. Let us picture a man under the influence of anger, and another man upon whom truth is acting as an inward light. The first man is frowning—why? In such cases the brow is knitted because an excessive force is working inwardly, like a poison, to hold down a surplus of egoism which would like to destroy everything that exists alongside and separate from the man himself. In the clenched fist of anger we see the wrathful self closed up in itself and refusing to go forth into the outer world. Now compare this with the facial expression of someone who is discovering truth. When he perceives the light of truth, he too may frown, but in his case the wrinkled brow is a means whereby the soul expands, as though it would like to grasp and absorb the whole world with devoted love. Observe, too, the eyes of a man who is trying to overhear the world's secrets. His eyes are shining, as though to encompass everything around him in the outer world. He is released from himself; his hand is not clenched, but held out with a gesture that seeks to absorb the being of the world.

The whole difference between anger and truth is thus expressed in human physiognomy and gesture. Anger thrusts the human being deeper into himself. If he strives for truth, his being expands into the outer world; and the more united he becomes with the outer world, the more he turns away from the truths gained by reflective thinking to those gained by creative thinking. Therefore, Goethe in his *Pandora* brings into opposition with each other certain characters who can be taken to represent forces at work in the human soul. They are intended to express symbolically the relationships between the characteristics and capacities of the soul.

When you open *Pandora,* you come upon something remarkable and highly significant at the very start. On the side of Prometheus, the stage is loaded with tools and implements constructed by man. In all these, human energies have been at work, but in a certain sense it is all rough and ready. On the side of Epimetheus, the other Titan, there is a complete contrast. Here everything is perfectly finished; we see not so much what man creates, but a bringing together of what Nature has already produced. It is all the result of reflective thinking. Here we have combination and shaping, a symmetrical ordering of Nature's work. On the side of Prometheus, unsymmetry and roughness; on the side of Epimetheus, elegant and harmonious products of Nature, culminating in a view of a wonderful landscape. What does all this signify? We need only consider the two contrasted characters: Prometheus the creative thinker, Epimetheus the reflective thinker. With Prometheus we find the products mainly of creative thinking. Here, although man's powers are limited and clumsy, he is productive. He cannot yet shape his creations as perfectly as Nature shapes her own; but they are all the outcome of his own powers and tools. He is also deficient in feeling for scenes of natural beauty.

On the side of Epimetheus, the reflective thinker, we see the heritage of the past, brought into symmetrical order by himself. And because he is a reflective thinker, we see in the background a beautiful landscape which gives its own special pleasure to the human eye. Epimetheus now comes forward and discloses his individual character. He explains that he is there to experience the past, and to reflect upon past occurrences and the visible world. But in his speech he reveals the dissatisfaction that this kind of attitude can at times call forth in the soul. He feels hardly any difference between day and night. In brief, the figure of Epimetheus shows us reflective thinking in its most extreme form. Then Prometheus comes forward carrying a torch and emerging from the darkness of night. Among his followers are smiths; they set to work on the man-made objects that are lying around, while Prometheus

The Mission of Truth

makes a remarkable statement that will not be misunderstood if we are alive to Goethe's meaning. The smiths extol productivity and welcome the fact that in the course of production many things have to be destroyed. In a one-sided way they extol fire. A man who is an all-round reflective thinker will not praise one thing at the expense of another. He casts his eye over the whole. Prometheus, however, says at once:

> In partiality let the active man
> Find his pleasure

He extols precisely the fact that to be active entails the acceptance of limitations. In Nature, the right is established when the wrong destroys itself. But to the smiths Prometheus says: Carry on doing whatever can be done. He is the creative man; he emerges with his torch from the darkness of night in order to show how from the depths of his soul the truth gained by his creative thinking comes forth. Unlike Epimetheus, he is far from a dreamlike feeling that night and day are all one. Nor does he experience the world as a dream. For his soul has been at work, and in its own dark night it has grasped the thoughts which now emerge from it. They are no dreams, but truths for which the soul has bled. By this means the soul advances into the world and gains release from itself; but at the same time it incurs the danger of losing itself. This does not yet apply to Prometheus himself, but when a man introduces one-sidedness into the world, the danger appears among his descendants.

Phileros, the son of Prometheus, is already inclined to love and cherish and enjoy the products of creative work, while his father Prometheus is still immersed in the stream of life's creative power. In Phileros we are shown the power of creative thinking developed in a one-sided way. He rushes out into life, not knowing where to search for enjoyment. Prometheus cannot pass on to his son his own fruitfully creative strength, and so Phileros appears incomprehensible to Epimetheus, who out of his own rich experience would like to counsel him on his headlong career.

We are then magnificently shown what mere reflective thinking involves. This is connected with the myth that Zeus, having fettered Prometheus to the rock, imposes Pandora, the all-gifted, on mankind.

> Most beautiful and gifted she approached
> The amazed watcher, moving with noble grace,
> Her gracious look inquiring whether I,
> Like to my sterner brother, would repel her,

> But all too strongly were my heart-beats stirred,
> With sense bemused my charming bride I welcomed.
> Towards the mysterious dowry then I turned,
> The earthen vessel, tall and shapely, stood
> Close-sealed...

Prometheus had warned his brother against this gift from the gods. But Epimetheus, with his different character, accepts the gift, and when the earthen vessel is opened, all the afflictions that can befall mankind come pouring out. Only one thing is left in the vessel—Hope.

Who, then, is Pandora and what does she signify? Truly a mystery of the soul is concealed in her. The fruits of reflective thinking are dead products, an abstract reflection of the mechanical thoughts forged by Hephaestus. This wisdom is powerless in the face of the universally creative wisdom from which the world has been born. What can this abstract reflection give to mankind?

We have seen how this kind of truth can be sterile and can lay waste the soul, and we can understand how all the afflictions that fall on mankind come pouring out of Pandora's vessel. In Pandora we have to see truth without the powers of creativity, the truth of reflective thinking, a truth which builds up a mechanised thought-picture in the midst of the world's creative life. For the mere reflective thinker only one thing remains. While the creative thinker unites his Ego with the future and gets free from himself, the reflective thinker can look to the future only with hope, for he has no part in shaping it. He can only hope that things will happen. Goethe shows his deep comprehension of the myth by endowing the marriage of Epimetheus and Pandora with two children: Elpore (Hope) and Epimeleia (Care), who safeguards existing things. In fact, man has in his soul two offspring of dead, abstract, mechanically conceived truth. This kind of truth is unfruitful and cannot influence the future; it can only reflect what is already there. It leaves a man with nothing but the hope that what is true will duly come to pass. This is represented by Goethe with splendid realism in the figure of Elpore, who, if someone asks her whether this or that is going to happen, always gives the same answer, Yes, yes. If a Promethean man were to stand before the world and speak of the future, he would say: "I hope for nothing. With my own forces I will shape the future." But a reflective thinker can only reflect on the past and hope for the future; thus Elpore, when asked whether this or that will happen, replies always, yes yes. We hear it again and again. In this way a daughter of reflective thinking is admirably characterised and her sterility is indicated.

The Mission of Truth

The other daughter of this reflective thinking, Epimeleia, is she who cares for existing things. She sets them all in symmetrical order and can add nothing from her own resources. But all things which fail to develop are increasingly liable to destruction; hence we see how anxiety about them continually mounts, and how through mere reflective thinking a destructive element finds its way into the world. This is wonderfully well indicated by Goethe when he makes Phileros fall in love with Epimeleia. We see him, burnt up with jealousy, pursuing Epimeleia, until she takes refuge from him with the Titan brothers. Strife and dissension come simultaneously on to the scene. Epimeleia complains that the person she loves is the very one to seek her life.

Everything that Goethe goes on to say shows how deeply he had penetrated into the effects of creative thinking and reflective thinking on the soul. The creative thinking of the smiths is set in wonderful contrast to the outlook of the shepherds; whilst the latter take what Nature offers, the former work on the products of Nature and transform them. Therefore Prometheus says of the shepherds: they are seeking peace, but they will not find a peace that satisfies their souls:

> Go your ways in peace; but peace
> You will not find.

For a wish merely to preserve things as they are leads only to the unproductive side of Nature.

The truths which belong to creative thinking and reflective thinking respectively are thus set before us in the figures of Prometheus and Epimetheus, and in all the characters connected with them. They represent those soul-forces which can spring from an excessive, one-sided predilection for one or other way of striving after truth. And after we have seen how disastrous are the consequences of these extremes, we are shown finally the one and only remedy—the co-operation of the Titan brothers. The drama leads on to an outbreak of fire in a property owned by Epimetheus. Prometheus, who is prepared to demolish a building if it no longer serves its purpose, advises his brother to make all speed to the spot and do all he can to halt the destruction. But Epimetheus no longer cares for that; he is thinking about Pandora and is lost in his recollection of her. Interesting also is a dialogue between the brothers about her:

> Prometheus:
> Her form sublime, from ancient dark emerging,
> Came near me also. To make another like her,
> Even Hephaestus would have failed in that.

Metamorphoses of the Soul

> Epimetheus:
> Art thou, too, prating of this fabled birth?
> From ancient gods, a mighty race, she springs:
> Uranione, Hera's peer, and sister
> Of Zeus himself.
>
> Prometheus:
> And yet Hephaestus, for her rich adornment,
> Made for her head a net of shining gold,
> Weaving with subtle hand the finest threads.

In every sentence spoken by Prometheus we see how mechanised, abstract limitations obsess his mind. Then Eos, the Dawn, appears. She is an unlit being who precedes and heralds the sun, but also contains its light within herself already. She does not simply emerge from the darkness of night; she represents a transition to something which has overcome night. Prometheus appears with his torch because he has just come out of the night. The artificial light he carries indicates how his creative work proceeds from the night's darkness. Epimetheus can indeed admire the sunlight and its gifts, but he experiences everything as in a dream. He is an example of pure reflective thinking. The way in which light can escape the attention of a soul absorbed in creative activity is shown by what Prometheus says in the light of day. His people, he says, are called upon not merely to observe the sun and the light, but to be themselves a source of illumination. Now Eos, Aurora, comes forward. She calls upon men to be active everywhere in doing right. Phileros, already having sought death, should unite with the forces which will make it possible for him to rescue himself. The smiths, who are working within the limits of their creative thinking, and the shepherds, who accept things as they are, are now joined by the fishermen. And we see how Eos gives them advice:

> Morning of youth, dawning of day,
> More beautiful than ever,
> From the unfathomed ocean
> I bring you now.
> Awake, shake off your sleep,
> You dwellers in the bay
> By cliffs encircled,
> You fishermen, arise,
> And ply your craft.
> With speed spread out your nets

The Mission of Truth

> Around the well-known waters,
> A splendid catch is certain
> When my voice cheers you on.
> Swim, you swimmers! Dive, you divers!
> Watch, you watchers on the heights!
> May the shores and seas together
> Swarm with swift abounding life!

Then we are shown in a wonderful way how Phileros is rescued on the surging flood and unites his own strength with the strength of the waves. The active creative power in him is thus united with the creative power in Nature. So the elements of Prometheus and Epimetheus are reconciled.

Thus Goethe offers a solution rich in promise, by showing how knowledge gained from Nature by reflective thinking can be fired with productive energy by the creative thinking element. This latter acquires its rightful strength by receiving, in loyalty to truth, what the gods "up there" bestow:

> Take note of this:
> What is desirable, you feel down here;
> What is to be given, they know up there.
> You Titans make a great beginning,
> But the way to the eternal good, the forever beautiful,
> That is the work of the gods; they ensure it.

The union of Prometheus and Epimetheus in the human soul will bring salvation for them and for mankind. The whole drama is intended to indicate that through an all-round grasping of truth the entire human race, and not only individuals, will find satisfaction. Goethe wished to show that an understanding of the real nature of truth will unite humanity and foster love and peace among men. Then Hope, also, is transformed in the soul—Hope who says yes to everything but is powerless to bring anything about. The poem was to have ended with the transformed Elpore, Elpore thraseia, coming forward to tell us that she is no longer a prophetess but is to be incorporated into the human soul, so that human beings would not merely cherish hopes for the future but would have the strength to co-operate in bringing about whatever their own productive power could create. To believe in the transformation wrought by truth upon the soul—that is the whole perfected truth which reconciles Prometheus and Epimetheus.

Metamorphoses of the Soul

Naturally, these sketchy indications can bring out only a little of all that can be drawn from the poem. The deep wisdom that called forth this fragment from Goethe will disclose itself first to those who approach it with the support of a spiritual-scientific way of thinking. They can experience a satisfying, redeeming power which flows out from the poem and quickens them.

We must not fail to mention a remarkably beautiful phrase that Goethe included in his *Pandora*. He says that the divine wisdom which flows into the world must work in harmony with all that we are able to achieve through our own Promethean power of creative thinking. The element that comes to meet us in the world and teaches us what wisdom is, Goethe called the Word. That which lives in the soul and must unite itself with the reflective thinking of Epimetheus, is the Deed of Prometheus. So the union of the Logos or Word with the Deed gives rise to the ideal that Goethe wished to set before us in his *Pandora* as the fruit of a life rich in experiences. Towards the end of the poem, Prometheus makes a remarkable statement: "A real man truely celebrates the deed." This is the truth that remains hidden from the reflective thinking element in the soul.

If we open ourselves to this whole poem, we can come to realise the heroic yearning for development felt by men such as Goethe, and the great modesty which prevents them from supposing that by reaching a certain stage they have done enough and need not try to go further. Goethe was an apprentice of life up to his last day, and always recognised that when a man has been enriched by an experience he must overcome what he has previously held to be true.

When as a young man, Goethe was beginning to work on *Faust,* and had occasion to introduce some translations from the Bible, he decided that the words "In the beginning was the Word", should be rendered as "In the beginning was the Deed". At this same time he wrote a fragment on Prometheus.[28] There we see the young Goethe as altogether active and Promethean, confident that simply by developing his own forces, not fructified by cosmic wisdom, he could progress. In his maturity, with a long experience of life behind him, he realised that it was wrong to underestimate the Word, and that Word and Deed must be united. In fact, Goethe revised parts of his *Faust* while he was writing his *Pandora*. We can understand how Goethe came by degrees to maturity only if we realise the nature of truth in all its forms.

It will always be good for man if he wrestles his way to realising that truth can be apprehended only by degrees. Or take a genuine, honest, all-round seeker after truth who is called upon to bring forcibly before the world some truth he has discovered. It will be very good if he

The Mission of Truth

reminds himself that he has no grounds for pluming himself on this one account. There are no grounds at any time for remaining content with something already known. On the contrary, such knowledge as we have gained from our considerations yesterday and today should lead us to feel that, although the human being must stand firmly on the ground of the truth he has acquired and must be ready to defend it, he must from time to time withdraw into himself, as Goethe did. When he does this, the forces arising from the consciousness of the truth he has gained will endow him with a feeling for the right standards and for the standpoint he should make his own. From the enhanced consciousness of truth we should ever and again withdraw into ourselves and say, with Goethe: Much that we once discovered and took for truth is now only a dream, a dreamlike memory; and what we think today, will not survive when we put it to a deeper test. The words often spoken by Goethe to himself in relation to his own honest search for truth may well be echoed by every man in his solitary hours:

> A poor wight am I
> Through and through.
> My thoughts miss the mark,
> My dreams, they are not true.[29]

If we can feel this, we shall be in the right relationship to our high ideal, Truth.

LECTURE 4
The Mission of Reverence

Berlin, 28th October, 1909

You all know the words with which Goethe concluded his life's masterpiece, *Faust*:

> All things transient
> Are but a parable;
> Earth's insufficiency
> Here finds fulfilment;
> The indescribable
> Here becomes deed;
> The eternal-feminine
> Draws us on high.

It goes without saying that in this context the "eternal-feminine" has nothing to do with man and woman. Goethe is making use of an ancient turn of speech. In all forms of mysticism—and Goethe gives these closing lines to a *Chorus mysticus*—we find an urge in the soul, at first quite indefinite, towards something which the soul has not yet come to know and to unite itself with, but must strive towards. This goal, at first only dimly surmised by the aspiring soul, is called by Goethe, in accord with the mystics of diverse times, the eternal-feminine, and the whole sense of the second part of *Faust* confirms this way of taking the concluding lines.

This *Chorus mysticus*, with its succinct words, can be set against the *Unio mystica*, the name given by true mystical thinkers to union with the eternal-feminine, far off spiritually but within human reach. When the soul has risen to this height and feels itself to be at one with the eternal-feminine, then we can speak of mystical union, and this is the highest summit that we shall be considering today.

In the last two lectures, on the mission of anger and the mission of

The Mission of Reverence

truth, we saw that the soul is involved in a process of evolution. On the one hand, we indicated certain attributes which the soul must strive to overcome, whereby anger, for example, can become an educator of the soul; and we saw on the other, how truth can educate the soul in its own special way.

The end and goal of this process of development cannot always be foreseen by the soul. We can place some object before us and say that it has developed from an earlier form to its present stage. We cannot say this of the human soul, for the soul is progressing through a continuing evolution in which it is itself the active agent. The soul must feel that, having developed to a certain point, it has to go further. And as a self-conscious soul it must say to itself: How is it that I am able to think not only about my development in the past but also about my development in the future?

Now we have often explained how the soul, with all its inner life, is composed of three members. We cannot go over this in detail again today, but it will be better to mention, it, so that this lecture can be studied on its own account. We call these three members of the soul the Sentient Soul, the Intellectual Soul and the Consciousness Soul. The Sentient Soul can live without being much permeated by thinking. Its primary role is to receive impressions from the outer world and to pass them on inwardly. It is also the vehicle of such feelings of pleasure and pain, joy and grief, as come from these outer impressions. All human emotions, all desires, instincts and passions arise from within the Sentient Soul. Man has progressed from this stage to higher levels; he has permeated the Sentient Soul with his thinking and with feelings induced by thinking. In the Intellectual Soul, accordingly, we do not find indefinite feelings arising from the depths, but feelings gradually penetrated by the inner light of thought. At the same time it is from the Intellectual Soul that we find emerging by degrees the human Ego, that central point of the soul which can lead to the real Self and makes it possible for us to purify, cleanse and refine the qualities of our soul from within, so that we can become the master, leader and guide of our volitions, feelings and thoughts.

This Ego, as we have seen already, has two aspects. One possibility of development for it is through the endeavours that man must make to strengthen this inner centre more and more, so that an increasingly powerful influence can radiate out from it into his environment and into all the life around him. To enhance the value of the soul for the surrounding world and at the same time to strengthen its independence —that is one aspect of Ego development.

The reverse side of this is egoism. A self that is too weak will lose

Metamorphoses of the Soul

itself in the flood of the world. But if a man likes to keep his pleasures and desires, his thinking and his brooding, all within himself, his Ego will be hardened and given over to self-seeking and egoism.

Now we have briefly described the content of the Intellectual Soul. We have seen how wild impulses, of which anger is an example, can educate the soul if they are overcome and conquered. We have seen also that the Intellectual Soul is positively educated by truth, when truth is understood as something that a man possesses inwardly and takes account of at all times; when it leads us out of ourselves and enlarges the Ego, while at the same time it strengthens the Ego and makes it more selfless.

Thus we have become acquainted with the means of self-education that are provided for the Sentient Soul and the Intellectual Soul. Now we have to ask: Is there a similar means provided for the Consciousness Soul, the highest member of the human soul? We can also ask: What is there in the Consciousness Soul which develops of its own accord, corresponding to the instincts and desires in the Sentient Soul? Is there something that belongs by nature to the Consciousness Soul, such that man could acquire very little of it if he were not already endowed with it?

There is something which reaches out from the Intellectual Soul to the Consciousness Soul—the strength and sagacity of thinking. The Consciousness Soul can come to expression only because man is a thinking being, for its task is to acquire knowledge of the world and of itself, and for this it requires the highest instrument of knowledge—thinking.

We learn about the external world through perceptions; they stimulate us to gain knowledge of our surroundings. To this end, we need only devote our attention to the outer world and not stand blankly in front of it, for then the outer world itself draws us on to satisfy our thirst for knowledge by observing it. With regard to gaining knowledge of the supersensible world, we are in a quite different situation. First of all, the supersensible world is not there in front of us. If a man wishes to gain a knowledge of it, so that this knowledge will permeate his Consciousness Soul, the impulse to do so must come from within and must penetrate his thinking through and through. This impulse can come only from the other powers of his soul, feeling and willing. Unless his thinking is stimulated by both these powers, it will never be impelled to approach the supersensible world. This does not mean that the supersensible is merely a feeling, but that feeling and willing must act as inner guides towards its unknown realm. What qualities, then, must feeling and willing acquire towards its unknown realm.

The Mission of Reverence

What qualities, then, must feeling and willing acquire in order to do this? First of all, someone might object to the use of a feeling as a guide to knowledge. But a simple consideration will show that in fact this is what feeling does. Anyone who takes knowledge seriously, will admit that in acquiring knowledge we must proceed logically. We use logic as an instrument for testing the knowledge we acquire. How, then, if logic is this instrument, can logic itself be proved? One might say: Logic can prove itself. Yes, but before we begin proving logic by logic, it must be at least possible to grasp logic with our feeling. Logical thought cannot be proved primarily by logical thought, but only by feeling. Indeed, everything that constitutes logic is first proved through feeling, by the infallible feeling for truth that dwells in the human soul. From this classical example we can see how feeling is the foundation of logic and of thinking. Feeling must give the impulse for the verification of thought. What must feeling become if it is to provide an impulse not only for thinking in general, but for thinking about worlds with which we are at first unacquainted and cannot survey?

Feeling of this kind must be a force which strives from within towards an object yet unknown. When the human soul seeks to encompass with feeling some other thing, we call this feeling love. Love can of course be felt for something known, and there are many things in the world for us to love. But as love is a feeling, and a feeling is the foundation of thinking in the widest sense, we must be clear that the unknown supersensible can be grasped by feeling before thinking comes in. Unprejudiced observation, accordingly, shows that it must be possible for human beings to come to love the unknown supersensible before they are able to conceive it in terms of thought. This love is indeed indispensable before the supersensible can be penetrated by the light of thought.

At this stage, also, the will can be permeated by a force which goes out towards the supersensible unknown. This quality of the will, which enables a man to wish to carry out his aims and intentions with regard to the unknown, is devotion. So can the will inspire devotion towards the unknown, while feeling becomes love of the unknown; and when these two emotions are united they together give rise to reverence in the true sense of the word. Then this devotion becomes the impulse that will lead us into the unknown, so that the unknown can be taken hold of by our thinking. Thus it is that reverence becomes the educator of the Consciousness Soul. For in ordinary life, also, we can say that when a man endeavours to grasp with his thinking some external reality not yet known to him, he will be approaching it with love and devotion. Never will the Consciousness Soul gain a knowledge of external objects unless love and devotion inspire its quest; otherwise the objects will not be truly observed. This also applies quite specially to all endeavours to gain knowledge of the supersensible world.

In all cases, however, the soul must allow itself to be educated by the Ego, the source of self-consciousness. We have seen how the Ego gains increasing independence and strength by overcoming certain soul qualities, such as anger, and by cultivating others, such as the sense of truth. After that, the self-education of the Ego comes to an end; its education through reverence begins. Anger is to be overcome and discarded; a sense of truth is to permeate the Ego; reverence is to flow from the Ego towards the object of which knowledge is sought. Thus, having raised itself out of the Sentient Soul and the Intellectual Soul by overcoming anger and other passions and by cultivating a sense of truth, the Ego is drawn gradually into the Consciousness Soul by the influence of reverence. If this reverence becomes stronger and stronger, one can speak of it as a powerful impulse towards the realm described by Goethe:

> All things transient
> Are but a parable;
> Earth's insufficiency
> Here finds fulfilment;
> The indescribable
> Here becomes deed;
> The eternal-feminine
> Draws us on high.

The soul is drawn by the strength of its reverence towards the eternal, with which it longs to unite itself. But the Ego has two sides. It is impelled by necessity to enhance continually its own strength and activity. At the same time it has the task of not allowing itself to fall under the hardening influence of egoism. If the Ego seeks to go further and gain knowledge of the unknown and the supersensible, and takes reverence as its guide, it is exposed to the immediate danger of losing itself. This is most likely to happen, above all, to a human being if his will is always submissive to the world. If this attitude gains increasingly the upper hand, the result may be that the Ego goes out of itself and loses itself in the other being or thing to which it has submitted. This condition can be likened to fainting by the soul, as distinct from bodily fainting. In bodily fainting the Ego sinks into undefined darkness; in fainting by the soul, the Ego loses itself spiritually while the bodily faculties and perceptions of the outer world are not impaired. This can

The Mission of Reverence

happen if the Ego is not strong enough to extend itself fully into the will and to guide it.

This self-surrender by the Ego can be the final result of a systematic mortification of the will. A man who pursues this course becomes incapable of willing or acting on his own account; he has surrendered his will to the object of his submissive devotion and has lost his own self. When this condition prevails, it produces an enduring impotence of the soul. Only when a devotional feeling is warmed through by the Ego, so that man can immerse himself in it without losing his Ego, can it be salutary for the human soul.

How, then, can reverence always carry the Ego with it? The Ego cannot allow itself to be led in any direction, as a human Self, unless it maintains in its thinking a knowledge of itself. Nothing else can protect the Ego from losing itself when devotion leads it out into the world. The soul can be led out of itself towards something external by the force of will, but when the soul leaves behind the boundary of the external, it must make sure of being illuminated by the light of thought.

Thinking itself cannot lead the soul out; this comes about through devotion, but thinking must then immediately exert itself to permeate with the life of thought the object of the soul's devotion. In other words, there must be a resolve to think about this object. Directly the devotional impulse loses the will to think, there is a danger of losing oneself. If anyone makes it a matter of principle not to think about the object of his devotion, this can lead in extreme cases to a lasting debility of the soul.

Is love, the other element in reverence, exposed to a similar fate? Something that radiates from the human Self towards the unknown must be poured into love, so that never for a moment does the Ego fail to sustain itself. The Ego must have the will to enter into everything which forms the object of its devotion, and it must maintain itself in face of the external, the unknown, the supersensible. What becomes of love if the Ego fails to maintain itself at the moment of encountering the unknown, if it is unwilling to bring the light of thinking and of rational judgment to bear on the unknown? Love of that kind becomes more sentimental enthusiasm (*Schwarmerei*). But the Ego can begin to find its way from the Intellectual Soul, where it lives, to the external unknown, and then it can never extinguish itself altogether . Unlike the will, the Ego cannot completely mortify itself. When the soul seeks to embrace the external world with feeling, the Ego is always present in the feeling, but if it is not supported by thinking and willing, it rushes forth without restraint, unconscious of itself. And if this love for the unknown is not accompanied by resolute thinking, the soul can

Metamorphoses of the Soul

fall into a sentimental extreme, somewhat like sleep-walking, just as the state reached by the soul when submissive devotion leads to loss of the Self is somewhat like a bodily fainting-fit. When a sentimental enthusiast goes forth to encounter the unknown, he leaves behind the strength of the Ego and takes with him only secondary forces. Since the strength of the Ego is absent from his consciousness, he tries to grasp the unknown as one does in the realm of dreams. Under these conditions the soul falls into what may be called an enduring state of dreaming or somnambulism.

Again, if the soul is unable to relate itself properly to the world and to other people, if it rushes out into life and shrinks from using the light of thought to illuminate its situation, then the Ego, having fallen into a somnambulistic condition, is bound to go astray and to wander through the world like a will-o-the-wisp.

If the soul succumbs to mental laziness and shuns the light of thought when it meets the unknown, then, and only then, will it harbour superstitions in one or other form. The sentimental soul, with its fond dreams, wandering through life as though asleep, and the indolent soul, unwilling to be fully conscious of itself—these are the souls most inclined to believe everything blindly. Their tendency is to avoid the effort of thinking for themselves and to allow truth and knowledge to be prescribed for them.

If we are to get to know an external object, we have to bring our own productive thinking to bear on it, and it is the same with the supersensible, whatever form this may take. Never, in seeking to gain a knowledge of the supersensible, must we exclude thinking. Directly we rely on merely observing the supersensible, we are exposed to all possible deceptions and errors. All such errors and superstitions, all the wrong or untruthful ways of entering the supersensible worlds, can be attributed in the last instance to a refusal to allow consciousness to be illuminated by the light of creative thought. No one can be deceived by information said to come from the spiritual world if he has the will to keep his thinking always active and independent. Nothing else will suffice, and this is something that every spiritual researcher will confirm. The stronger the will is to creative thinking, the greater is the possibility of gaining true, clear and certain knowledge of the spiritual world.

Thus we see the need for a means of education which will lead the Ego into the Consciousness Soul and will guide the Consciousness Soul in the face of the unknown, both the physical unknown and the unknown supersensible. Reverence, consisting of devotion and love, provides the means we seek. When the latter are imbued with the right kind of self-feeling, they become steps which lead to ever-greater heights.

The Mission of Reverence

True devotion, in whatever form it is experienced by the soul, whether through prayer or otherwise, can never lead anyone astray. The best way of learning to know something is to approach it first of all with love and devotion. A healthy education will consider especially how strength can be given to the development of the soul through the devotional impulse. To a child the world is largely unknown: if we are to guide him towards knowledge and sound judgment of it, the best way is to awaken in him a feeling of reverence towards it; and we can be sure that by so doing we shall lead him to fullness of experience in any walk of life.

It is very important for the human soul if it can look back to a childhood in which devotion, leading on to reverence, was often felt. Frequent opportunities to look up to revered persons, and to gaze with heartfelt devotion at things that are still beyond its understanding, provide a good impulse for higher development in later life. A person will always gratefully remember those occasions, when as a child in the family circle, he heard of some outstanding personality of whom everyone spoke with devotion and reverence. A feeling of holy awe, which gives reverence a specially intimate character, will then permeate the soul. Or someone may relate how with trembling hand, later on, he rang the bell and shyly made his way into the room of the revered personality whom he was meeting for the first time, after having heard him spoken of with so much respectful admiration. Simply to have come into his presence and exchanged a few words can confirm a devotion which will be particularly helpful when we are trying to unravel the great riddles of existence and are seeking for the goal which we long to make our own. Here reverence is a force which draws us upward, and by so doing fortifies and invigorates the soul. How can this be? Let us consider the outward expression of reverence in human gestures—what forms does it take? We bend our knees, fold our hands, and incline our heads towards the object of our reverence. These are the organs whereby the Ego, and above all the higher faculties of the soul, can express themselves most intensively.

In physical life a man stands upright by firmly extending his legs; his Ego radiates out through his hands in acts of blessing; and by moving his head he can observe the earth or the heavens. But from studying human nature, we learn also that our legs are stretched out at their best in strong, conscious action if they have first learnt to bend the knee where reverence is really strong, conscious action if they have first learnt to bend the knee where reverence is really due. For this genuflextion opens the door to a force which seeks to find its way into our organism. Knees which have not learnt to bend in reverence give

Metamorphoses of the Soul

out only what they have always had; they spread out their own nullity, to which they have added nothing. But legs which have learnt to genuflect receive, when they are extended, a new force, and then it is this, not their own nullity, which they spread around them. Hands which would fain bless and comfort, although they have never been folded in reverence and devotion, cannot bestow much love and blessing from their own nullity. But hands which have learnt to fold themselves in reverence have received a new force and are powerfully penetrated by the Ego. For the path taken by this force leads first through the heart, where it kindles love; and the reverence of the folded hands, having passed through the heart and flowed into the hands, turns into blessing.

The head may turn its eyes and strain its ears to survey the world in all directions, but it presents nothing but its own emptiness. If, however, the head has been bent in reverence, it gains a new force; it will bring to meet the outer world the feelings it has acquired through reverence.

Anyone who studies the gestures of people, and knows what they signify, will see how reverence is expressed in external physiognomy; he will see how this reverence enhances the strength of the Ego and so makes it possible for the Ego to penetrate into the unknown. Moreover, this self-education through reverence has the effect of raising to the surface our obscure instincts and emotions, our sympathies and antipathies, which otherwise make their way into the soul unconsciously or subconsciously, unchallenged by the light of judgment. Precisely these feelings are cleansed and purified through self-education by reverence and through the penetration by the Ego of the higher members of the soul. The obscure forces of sympathy and antipathy, always prone to error, are permeated by the light of the soul and transformed into judgment, aesthetic taste and rightly guided moral feeling. A soul educated by reverence will convert its dark cravings and aversions into a feeling for the beautiful and a feeling for the good. A soul that has cleansed its obscure instincts and will-impulses through devotion will gradually build up from them what we call moral ideals. Reverence is something that we plant in the soul as a seed; and the seed will bear fruit.

Human life offers yet another example. We see everywhere that the course of a man's life goes through ascending and declining stages. Childhood and youth are stages of ascent; then comes a pause, and finally, in the later years, a decline. Now the remarkable thing is, that the qualities acquired in childhood and youth reappear in a different form during the years of decline. If much reverence, rightly guided, has been part of the experience of childhood, it acts as a seed which comes

The Mission of Reverence

to fruition in old age as strength for active living. A childhood and youth during which devotion and love were not fostered under the right guidance will lead to a weak and powerless old age. Reverence must take hold of every soul that is to make progress in its development. How is it, then, with the corresponding quality in the object of our reverence? If we look with love on another being, then the reciprocated love of the latter will reveal what can perhaps arise. If a man is lovingly devoted to his God, he can be sure that God inclines to him also in love. Reverence is the feeling he develops for whatever he calls his God out there in the universe. Since the reaction to reverence cannot itself be called reverence, we may not speak of a divine reverence towards man. What, then, precisely is the opposite of reverence in this context? What is it that flows out to meet reverence when reverence seeks the divine? It is *might,* the Almighty power of the Divine. Reverence that we learn to feel in youth returns to us as strength for living in old age, and if we turn in reverence to the divine, our reverence flows back to us as an experience of the Almighty. That is what we feel, whether we look up to the starry heavens in their endless glory and our reverence goes out to all that lies around us, beyond our compass, or whether we look up to our invisible God, in whatever form, who pervades and animates the cosmos.

We look up towards the Almighty and we come to feel with certainty that we cannot advance towards union with that which is above us unless we first approach it from below with reverence. We draw nearer to the Almighty when we immerse ourselves in reverence. Thus we can speak of an Almighty in this sense, while a true feeling for the meaning of words prevents us from speaking of an All-loving. Power can be increased or enhanced in proportion to the number of beings over which it extends. It is different with love. If a child is loved by its mother, this does not prevent her from loving equally her second, third or fourth child. It is false for anyone to say: I must divide up my love because it is to cover two objects. It is false to speak either of an "all-knowledge" or of an indefinite "all-love". Love has no degree and cannot be limited by figures.

Love and devotion together make up reverence. We can have a devoted attitude to this or that unknown if we have the right feeling for it. Devotion can be enhanced, but it does not have to be divided up or multiplied when it is felt for a number of beings. Since this is true also of love, the Ego has no need to lose or disperse itself if it turns with love and devotion towards the unknown. Love and devotion are thus the right guides to the unknown, and the best educators of the soul in its advance from the Intellectual Soul to the Consciousness

Soul.

Whereas the overcoming of anger educates the Sentient Soul, and the striving for truth educates the Intellectual Soul, reverence educates the Consciousness Soul, bringing more and more knowledge within its reach. But this reverence must be led and guided from a standpoint which never shuts out the light of thought. When love flows forth from us, it ensures by its own worth that our Self can go with it, and this applies also to devotion. We could indeed lose our Self, but we need not. That is the point, and it must be kept especially in mind if an impulse of reverence enters into the education of the young. A blind, unconscious reverence is never right. The cultivation of reverence must go together with the cultivation of a healthy Ego-feeling.

Whereas the mystics of all ages, together with Goethe, have spoken of the unknown, undefined element to which the soul is drawn, as the eternal-feminine, we may without misunderstanding, speak of the element which must always animate reverence as the eternal-masculine. For just as the eternal-feminine is present in both man and woman, so is this eternal-masculine, this healthy Ego-feeling, present in all reverence by man or woman. And when Goethe's *Chorus mysticus* comes before us, we may, having come to know the mission of reverence which leads us towards the unknown, add the element which must permeate all reverence—the Eternal-masculine.

Thus we are now able to reach a right understanding of the experience of the human soul when it strives to unite itself with the unknown and attains to the *Unio mystica,* wherein all reverence is consummated.

But this mystical union will harm the soul if the Ego is lost while seeking to unite itself with the unknown in any form. If the Ego has lost itself, it will bring to the unknown nothing of value. Self-sacrifice in the *Unio mystica* requires that one must have become something, must have something to sacrifice. If a weak Ego, with no strength in itself, is united with what lies above us, the union has no value. The *Unio mystica* has value only when a strong Ego ascends to the regions of which the *Chorus mysticus* speaks. When Goethe speaks of the regions to which the higher reverence can lead us, in order to gain there the highest knowledge, and when his *Chorus mysticus* tells us in beautiful words:

> All things transient
> Are but a parable;
> Earth's insufficiency
> Here finds fulfilment;

The Mission of Reverence

The indescribable
Here becomes deed;
The eternal-feminine
Draws us on high—

Then, if we rightly understand the *Unio mystica,* we can reply: Yes—

All things transient
Are but a parable;
Earth's insufficiency
Here finds fulfilment;
The indescribable
Here becomes deed;
The eternal-masculine
Draws us on high.

LECTURE 5
Human Character

Munich, 14th March, 1909

The words written by Goethe after contemplating Schiller's skull can make a deep impression on the human soul. Goethe was present when Schiller's body was removed from its provisional grave and taken to the princely vault at Weimar. Holding Schiller's skull in his hands, Goethe believed he could recognise in the form and cast of this wonderful structure the whole nature of Schiller's spiritual being, and he was inspired to write these beautiful lines:

> What greater gift can life on man bestow
> Than that to him God-Nature should disclose
> How solid to spirit it attenuates,
> How spirit's work it hardens and preserves.[30]

Anyone who understands Goethe's feelings on this occasion will easily turn his mind to all those phenomena where something inward is working to reveal itself in material form, in plastic shapes, as drawing, and so on. We have a most eminent example of this shaping, whereby an inner being reveals itself through outward form, in what we call human character. For human character gives the most varied and manifold expression to the direction and purpose of man's life. We think of human character as having a basic consistency. Indeed, we feel that character is inseparable from a person's whole being, and that something has gone wrong if their thinking, feeling and doing do not make up in some way a harmonious unity. We speak of a split in a man's character as evidence of a real fault in his nature. If in private life a man upholds some principle or ideal, and then in public life says something contrary to it or at least discrepant, we speak of a break in his character, of his inner life falling apart. And we know very well that this can bring a man into difficult situations or may even wreck his

Human Character

life. The significance of a divided character is indicated by Goethe in a remarkable saying that he assigns to Faust—a saying that is often wrongly interpreted by people who believe that Goethe's innermost intentions are known to them:

> Two souls, alas, are pent within my breast,
> To tear themselves apart, forever striving;
> One, in pursuit of passions' crude delights,
> Clings close with avid senses to the world;
> The other, thrusting earthly dust away,
> Aspires to rise to longed-for higher realms.[31]

This divided condition of the soul is often spoken of as though it were a desirable achievement, but Goethe certainly does not say so. On the contrary, the passage shows clearly how unhappy Faust feels in that period under the pressure of these two drives, one aspiring towards ideal heights, the other striving towards the earthly. An unsatisfying state of soul which Faust has to overcome—that is what Goethe is describing. It is wrong to cite this schism in human nature as though it were justified; it is something to be abolished by the unified character that we must always strive to achieve.

If now we wish to look more deeply into human character, the facts outlined in previous lectures must be kept in mind. We must remember that the human soul, embracing the inner life of man, is not merely a chaos of intermingled feelings, instincts, concepts, passions and ideals, but has three distinct members—the Sentient Soul, the lowest; in the middle the Intellectual Soul; and finally the highest, the Consciousness Soul. These three soul-members are to be clearly distinguished, but they must not be allowed to fall apart, for the human soul must be a unity. What is it, then that holds them together? It is what we call the Ego in its true sense, the bearer of self-consciousness; the active element within our soul which plays upon its three members as a man plays upon the strings of an instrument. And the harmony or disharmony which the Ego calls forth by playing on the three soul-members is the basis of human character.

The Ego is indeed something of an inner musician, who with a powerful stroke calls one or other soul-member into activity; and the effects of their combined influence, resounding from within a human being as harmony or disharmony, make up the real foundation of his character.

However, that is no more than an abstract description. If we are to understand how character comes out in people, we must enter somewhat

Metamorphoses of the Soul

more deeply into human life and the being of man. We must show how the harmonious or disharmonious play of the Ego on the three soul-members sets its stamp on man's entire personality as he stands before us, and how personality is outwardly revealed.

Human life—as we all know—alternates between waking and sleeping. At night, when a man falls asleep, his feelings, his pleasure and pain, his joys and griefs, his urges, desires and passions, his perceptions and concepts, his ideas and ideals, all sink down into indefinite darkness; and his inner life passes into an unconscious or subconscious condition. What has happened?

As we have often explained, when a man goes to sleep his physical and etheric bodies remain in bed, while his astral body, including the Sentient Soul, Intellectual Soul and Consciousness Soul, withdraw, as does the Ego. During sleep the astral body and Ego are in a spiritual world. Why does a man return every night to this spiritual world? Why does he have to leave behind his physical and etheric bodies? There are good reasons for it. Spiritual Science says that the astral body is the bearer of pleasure and pain, joy and grief, instincts, desires and passions. Yes, but these are precisely the experiences that sink into indefinite darkness on going to sleep. Yet is it asserted that the astral body and the Ego are in spiritual worlds? Is there not a contradiction here?

Well, the contradiction is only apparent. The astral body is indeed the bearer of pleasure and pain, of joy and sorrow, of all the inner experiences that surge up and down in the soul during waking hours, but in man as he is today, the astral body cannot perceive these experiences directly. It can perceive them only when they are reflected from outside itself, and for this to be possible the Ego and astral body must come back into the etheric and physical bodies at the time of awakening from sleep. Everything that a man experiences inwardly, his pleasure and pain, joy and sorrow, is reflected by the physical and etheric bodies—especially by the etheric body—as from a mirror. But we must not suppose that this active process, which goes on every day from morning to evening, requires no effort to sustain it. The inner self of man, his Ego and astral body, his Consciousness Soul, Intellectual Soul and Sentient Soul, all have to work on the physical and etheric bodies, so that through the reciprocal interaction of his inner forces and his outer bodies the surging life of the daytime is engendered.

This reciprocal interaction involves a continual using up of soul-forces. When in the evening a man feels tired, this means that he is no longer able to draw from his inner life a sufficiency of the forces which enable him to work on his physical and etheric bodies. When he is nearing sleep and the faculty that required the most intensive play of

Human Character

his spirit into the physical, the faculty of speech, begins to weaken; when sight, smell, taste and finally hearing, the most spiritual of the senses, gradually fade away, because he is no longer able to draw on his inner forces to sustain them—then we see how these forces are used up through the day.

What is the origin of these forces? They come from the nightly condition of sleep. During the period between going to sleep and waking up the soul absorbs to the full the forces it needs for conjuring up before us all that we live through by day. During waking hours the soul can deploy its powers, but it cannot draw on the forces necessary for recuperation. Naturally, Spiritual Science is familiar with the various theories advanced by external science to account for the replenishment of forces used up by day, but we need not go into that now. Thus we can say that when the soul passes back from sleep into waking life, it brings from its spiritual home the forces which it devotes all day long to building up the soul-life which it conjures before us.

Now let us ask: When the soul goes off to sleep in the evening, does it carry anything with it into the spiritual world? Yes; and if we want to understand what this is, we must above all closely observe man's personal development between birth and death. This development is evident when in later years a man shows himself to be riper, richer in experience and wisdom learnt from life, while he may also have acquired certain capabilities and powers that he did not possess in his younger days.

A man does indeed receive from the outer world something that he transforms inwardly, as the following consideration clearly shows. Between 1770 and 1815 certain events of great significance for the development of the world took place. They were witnessed by the most diverse contemporaries, some of whom were unaffected by them, while others were so deeply moved that they became imbued with experience and wisdom and their soul-lives progressed to a higher stage.

How did this come about? It is best illustrated by a simple event in ordinary human life. Take the process of learning to write. What really happens before the moment when we are able to put pen to paper and express our thoughts in writing? A great deal must have happened— a whole series of experiences, from the first attempt to hold the pen, then to making the first stroke, and so on through all the efforts which lead at last to a grasp of the craft of writing. If we recall everything that must have occurred during months or years, and all we went through, perhaps by way of punishments and reproofs, until at last these experiences were transformed into knowing how to write, then

Metamorphoses of the Soul

we must say: These experiences were recast and remoulded, so that later on they appear like the essential core of what we call the ability to write.

Spiritual Science shows how this transformation comes about. It is possible only because human beings pass repeatedly through the condition of sleep. In daily life we find that when we are at pains to absorb something, the process of imprinting and retentions is considerably aided if we sleep on it; in that way we make it our own. The experiences we go through have to be united with the soul and worked on by the soul if they are to coalesce and be transformed into faculties. This whole process is carried through by the soul during sleep, and thereby our life is enhanced.

Present-day consciousness has little inkling of these things, but in times of ancient clairvoyance they were well known. An example will show how a poet once indicated in a remarkable way his knowledge of this transforming process. Homer, who can rightly be called a seer, describes in his Odyssey[32] how Penelope, during the absence of her husband, Odysseus, was besieged by a throng of suitors. She promised them that she would give her decision when she had completed a robe she was weaving; but every night she undid the work of the day. If a poet wishes to indicate how a series of experiences, such as those of Penelope with her suitors, are *not* to merge into a faculty—in this case the faculty of decision—he must show how these experiences have to be unwoven at night, or they would unfailingly coalesce.

To anyone imbued with a typical modern consciousness these ideas may sound like hair-splitting, or they may seem to be imposing something arbitrary on the poet; but the only really great men are those, whose work derives from the great world-secrets, and many people today who talk glibly of originality and the like have no inkling of the depths from which the truly great achievements in the arts have been born.

If now we look further at the progress of human life between birth and death, we have to recognise that it is confined within certain narrow limits. We can indeed work at and enhance our faculties; in later life we can acquire qualities of soul which were lacking earlier on; but all this is subject to the fact that we can accomplish nothing that would require us to transform our physical and etheric bodies. These bodies, with their particular aptitudes, are there at birth; we find them ready-made. For example, we can reach a certain understanding of music only if we are born with a musical ear. That is a crude example, but it shows how transformation can be frustrated; in such cases the experiences can indeed be united with the soul, but we must renounce any hope of weaving them into our bodily life.

Human Character

If, then, we consider human life from a higher standpoint, the possibility of breaking free from the physical body and laying it aside must be regarded as enormously wholesome and significant for our entire human existence. Our capacity to transform experiences into faculties is limited by the fact that every morning, on returning from sleep, we find our physical and etheric bodies waiting for us. At death we lay them aside and pass through the gate of death into a spiritual world. There, unhampered by these bodies, we can carry to spiritual completion those experiences between birth and death that we could not embody because of our corporeal limitations.

When we descend once more from the spiritual world to a new life on earth, then, and only then, can we take the powers we have woven into our spiritual archetype and give them physical existence by impressing them plastically into the initially soft human body. Now for the first time we can weave into our being those fruits of experience that we had indeed garnered in our previous life but could not then carry into physical embodiment. Seen in this light, death provides for the enhancement of life.

Moreover, this comparatively crude work that a man can do on his physical body, whereby he moulds into it what he could not impress on it in his previous life, is not the only possibility open to him. He is able also to imprint on his entire being certain finer fruits of foregoing lives.

When someone is born, his Ego and astral body, including his Sentient Soul, Intellectual Soul and Consciousness Soul, are by no means featureless; they are endowed with definite attributes and characteristics brought from previous lives. The cruder work, whereby the fruits of past experiences are impressed on the plastic physical body, is accomplished before birth, but a more delicate work—and this distinguishes man from the animals—is performed after birth. Throughout childhood and youth a man works into the finer organisation of his inner and outer nature certain determining characteristics and motives for action, brought by his Ego from a previous life. While the Ego thus impresses itself from within on its vehicles of expression, the fact of its activity and its way of working combine to form the character which a man presents to the world. Between birth and death the Ego works on the organs of the soul, the Sentient Soul, Intellectual Soul and Consciousness Soul, in such a way that they respond to what it has made of itself. But the Ego does not stand apart from the urges, desires and passions of the Sentient Soul. No, it unites itself with these emotions as though they were its own; and equally unites itself with the cognitions and the knowledge that belong to the Consciousness Soul.

Metamorphoses of the Soul

So it is, that the harmony or disharmony that a human being has wrought in his soul-members is impressed by his Ego on his exterior being in his next earthly life. Human character, therefore, although it appears to us as determined and inborn, can yet be seen to be developing gradually in the course of his life.

With animals, character is determined entirely at birth; an animal cannot work plastically on its exterior nature. Man has the advantage of appearing at birth with no definite character manifest externally, but in the depths of his being he has slumbering powers brought from previous lives; they work into his undeveloped exterior and gradually shape his character, in so far as this is determined by previous lives.

Thus we see how in a certain sense man has an inborn character, but one that gradually develops in the course of life. If we keep this in mind, we can understand how even eminent personalities can go wrong in judging character. There are philosophers who argue that character is inwardly determined and cannot change, but that is a mistake. It applies only to attributes which derive from a previous life and appear as inborn character. Man's inward centre, his Ego, sends out its influence and gives a common stamp and character to every member of his organism. This character extends into the soul and even into the external limbs of the body. We see this inner centre pouring itself forth, as it were, shaping everything in accord with itself, and we feel how this centre holds the members of the human organism together. Even in the external parts of his physical body the imprint of a man's inner being can be discerned.

In this connection, an artist once gave wonderful expression to something which generally receives only theoretical attention. The work he produced portrays human nature at the moment when the human Ego, the centre which holds the organism together as a unity, is lost, and the limbs, each going its own way, strain apart in different directions. The work I mean seizes precisely this moment, when a man loses the foundation of his character, of his being as a whole. But this work, a great and famous one, has been very often misunderstood. Do not suppose that I am about to level cheap criticism at men for whose work I have the highest respect. But the fact that even great minds can make mistakes in face of certain phenomena, just when they are most earnestly striving for truth, shows how difficult the path to truth really is.

One of the greatest German authorities on art, Winckelmann,[33] was impelled by his whole disposition to err in interpreting the work of art known as the Laocoon.[34] His interpretation has been widely admired. In many circles it has been thought that nothing better could

Human Character

be said about this portrayal of Laocoon, the Trojan priest who, with his two sons, was crushed to death by serpents. Winckelmann, filled with enthusiasm for this example of the sculptor's art, said that here we are shown how the priest, Laocoon, whose every limb bespeaks his nobility and greatness, is torn with anguish, above all the anguish of a father. He is placed between his two sons, with the serpents coiled round their bodies. Conscious of the pain inflicted on his sons, he himself, as a father, is so agonised by it that the lower part of his body is contracted, as though pressing out the full degree of pain. He forgets himself, consumed with immeasurable pity for his sons.

This is a beautiful explanation of a father's ordeal, but if—just because we honour Winckelmann as a great personality—we look repeatedly and conscientiously at the Laocoon, we are obliged finally to say that Winckelmann must be mistaken, for it is not possible for pity to be the dominating motif in the scene portrayed. The father's head is aligned at such an angle that he cannot see his sons. Winckelmann's view of the group is quite wrong. The immediate impression we get from looking at the figures is that here we are witnessing the quite definite moment when the encircling pressure of the snakes has driven the human Ego out of Laocoon's body, and the separate instincts, deprived of the Ego, make their way into the physical body. Thus we see the head, the lower body and the limbs each taking its own course, not brought into natural harmony with the figure as a whole because the Ego is absent. The Laocoon group shows us, in external bodily terms, how a man loses his unified character when bereft of the Ego, the strong central point which holds together the members of his bodily organism. And if we allow this spectacle to work on our souls, we can come to experience the unifying element which naturally expresses itself in the harmonising of the limbs, and imprints on a man what we call his character.

But now we must ask: If it is true that a man's character is to some extent inborn—if the characteristics given by birth cannot by any effort be altered beyond a certain limit, as every glance at human life will tell us—is it then possible for a man to change his character in a certain way?

Yes, in so far as character belongs to the life of the soul and is not subject to the bodily limitations we encounter every morning on waking from sleep, and so can help to harmonise and strengthen the Sentient Soul, Intellectual Soul and Consciousness Soul. To this extent there can be a development of character during a person's life between birth and death.

Some knowledge of all this is of special importance in education. Essential as it is to understand the temperaments and the differences between them, it is necessary also to know something about human character and what can be done to change it between birth and death, even though it is in some measure determined by the fruits of a previous life. If we are to make good use of this knowledge, we must be clear that personal life goes through four typical periods of development. In my small book, *The Education of the Child in the Light of Anthroposophy,* you will find further information on these stages; here I can only sketch them in outline.

The first period runs from birth up to the beginning of the change of teeth around the age of seven. It is during this period that external influence can do most to develop the physical body. During the next period, from the seventh year up to the onset of puberty at about the thirteenth, fourteenth or fifteenth year, the etheric body, particularly, can be developed. Then comes a third period when the lower astral body, especially, can be developed, until finally, from about the 21st year onwards, the time comes when a human being meets the world as a free, independent being and can himself work on the progress of his soul.

The years from 20 to 28 are important for developing the forces of the Sentient Soul. The next seven years up to the age of 35—these are all only average figures—are important for the development of the Intellectual Soul, especially through intercourse with the outer world.

All this may be regarded as nonsense by those who fail to observe the course of human life, but anyone who studies life with open eyes will come to know that certain elements in the human being are most open to development during particular periods. During our early twenties we are particularly well placed to bring our desires, instincts, passions and so on into relation with the impressions and influences received from our dealings with the outer world. We can feel our powers growing through the corresponding interaction between the Intellectual Soul and the world around us, and anyone who knows what true knowledge is, will realise that all earlier acquisitions of knowledge were no more than a preparation for this later stage. The ripeness of experience which enables one to survey and evaluate the knowledge one acquires is not attained, on average, before the thirty-fifth year. These laws exist. Anyone unwilling to recognise them is unwilling to observe the course of human life.

If we keep this in mind, we can see how human life between birth and death is structured. The work of the Ego in harmonising the soul-members, and its necessary endeavour to impress the fruits of its work on the physical body, will show you how important it is for an educator to know how the physical body goes through its development up to the seventh year. It is only during this period that influences from the outer world can be brought in to endow the physical body with power and strength. And here we encounter a mysterious connection between the physical body and the Consciousness Soul, a connection which exact observation can thoroughly confirm.

If the Ego is to gain strength, so that in later life, after the thirty-fifth year, it can permeate itself with the forces of the Consciousness Soul, and through this permeation can go forth to acquire knowledge of the world, it ought to encounter no boundaries in the physical body. For the physical body can set up the greatest obstacles to the Consciousness Soul and the Ego, if the Ego is not content to remain enclosed in the inner life but wishes to go out and engage in free intercourse with the world. Now since in bringing up a child during his first seven years we are able to strengthen the forces of his physical body, within certain limits, a remarkable connection between two periods of life is apparent. What can be accomplished for a child during these years by those who care for him is not a matter of indifference! People who fail to realise this have not learnt how to observe human life. Anyone who can compare the early years of childhood with the period after the thirty-fifth year will know that if a man is to go out into the world and engage in free intercourse with it, the best thing we can do for him is to bring him the right sort of influence during his early years. Anything we can do to help the child to find joy in immediate physical life, and to feel that love surrounds him, will strengthen the forces of his physical body, making it supple, pliant and open to education. The more joy, love and happiness that we can give the child during his early years, the fewer obstacles and hindrances he will encounter later on, when the work of his Ego on his Consciousness Soul should enable him to become an open character, associating in free give-and-take with the outer world. Anything in the way of unkindness pain or distressing circumstances that we allow the child to suffer up to his seventh year has a hardening effect on his physical body, and this creates obstacles for him in later life. He will tend to become a closed character, a man whose whole being is imprisoned in his soul, so that he is unable to achieve a free and open intercourse with the world and the impressions it yields.

Again, there are connections between the etheric body and the second period of life, and therefore with the Intellectual Soul. The play of the Ego on the Intellectual Soul releases forces which can either endow a man with courage and initiative or incline him to cowardice, indecision, sluggishness. Which way it goes depends on the strength of the Ego. But when a man has the best opportunity to use the Intellec-

Metamorphoses of the Soul

tual Soul for strengthening his character through intercourse with the world, between the ages of 28 and 35, he may encounter hindrances in his etheric body. If during the period from the seventh to the fourteenth year we supply the etheric body with forces that will prevent it from creating these hindrances in later life, we shall be doing something for his education that should earn his gratitude.

If during the period from seven to fourteen in a child's life we can stand towards him as an authority, and as a source of truth whom he can trust, this is particularly health-giving. Through this relationship, we, as parents or teachers, can strengthen his etheric forces so that in later life he will encounter the least possible obstacles in his etheric body. Then he will be able, if his Ego has the disposition for it, to become a man of courage and initiative. If we are aware of these hidden connections, we can have an enormously health-giving influence on human beings while they are growing up.

Our chaotic education has lost all knowledge of these connections; they were known instinctively in earlier times. It is always a pleasure to see that some old teachers knew of these things, whether by instinct or by inspiration. Rotteck's old *World History,* for example: it was to be found in our fathers' libraries and it may now be out of date here and there, but if we approach it with understanding we encounter a quite individual method of presentation which shows that Rotteck, who taught history in Freiburg, had a way of teaching which was the very reverse of dry or insipid. We have only to read the Foreword, which is quite out of the ordinary in spirit, to feel; here is a man who knows that in addressing young people of this age—from 14 to 21, when the astral body is developing—he must bring them into touch with the power of great, beautiful ideals. Rotteck is always at pains to show how we can be inspired by the great thoughts of the heroes and to kindle the enthusiasm that can be felt for all that men and women have striven for and suffered in the course of human evolution.

This approach is entirely justified, for the influence thus poured into the astral body during these years is of direct benefit to the Sentient Soul, when the Ego is working to develop a person's character through free intercourse with the world. All that has flowed into the soul from high ideals and enthusiasm is imprinted on the Sentient Soul and embodied accordingly in character.

Thus we see that because the physical, etheric and astral bodies are still plastic in young people, this or that influence can be impressed on them through education, and this makes it possible for a man to work on his character in later life. If education has not helped him in this way, he will find it difficult to work on his character and he will have

Human Character

to resort to the strongest measures. He will need to devote himself to deep meditative contemplation of certain qualities and feelings in order to impress them consciously on his soul. He must try, for example, to experience inwardly the content of those religious confessions which can speak to us as more than theories. He must devote himself again and again to contemplation of those great philosophies in the widest sense which in later life can lead through our thoughts and feelings into the great, all-embracing cosmic secrets. If we can immerse ourselves in these secrets, ever and again willingly devoting ourselves to them; if through daily prayer we make them part of ourselves, then through the play of the Ego, we can remould our characters in later life.

In this connection the essential thing is that the qualities acquired by and embodied in the Ego are imprinted on the Sentient Soul, the Intellectual Soul and the Consciousness Soul. Generally speaking, man has little power over his external body. We have seen how he encounters a boundary in his physical body, with its innate predispositions. Nevertheless, observation shows that in spite of this limitation, man can do some work on his physical body between birth and death.

Who has not noticed that a man who devotes himself for a decade to knowledge of a really deep kind—knowledge that does not remain grey learning but is transformed into pleasure and pain, happiness and sorrow, thus becoming real knowledge and uniting itself with the Ego—who has not noticed that such a man's physiognomy, his gestures, his entire behaviour have changed, showing how the working of the Ego has penetrated right into his external physique!

However, the extent to which the outer body can be influenced by powers acquired between birth and death is very limited. For the most part man has to resign himself to keeping them for his next earthly life.

On the other hand, the various attributes brought over from previous lives can be enhanced by working on them between birth and death, if the faculty for doing so has been acquired.

Thus we see how character is not confined to the inner life of the soul, but penetrates into a man's external physique and limbs. It finds expression, first, in his gestures; second, in his physiognomy; and third, in the plastic formation of the skull, the origin of what we call phrenology.

How, then, does character achieve this outward expression in gesture, physiognomy and bone-formation? The Ego works formatively first of all in the Sentient Soul, which embraces all the instincts, desires, passions—in short, everything that belongs to the inner impulses of the will. The note sounded by the Ego on this member of the soul is

Metamorphoses of the Soul

manifest externally as gesture, and this play of gestures, springing from a man's inner being, can tell us a great deal about his character.

When the Ego is active chiefly in the Sentient Soul, the note it sounds there resonates in the Intellectual Soul and the Consciousness Soul, and this, too, is evident in gesture. The coarser elements of the Sentient Soul come to expression in gestures connected with the lower part of the body. If, for instance, a man pats his stomach with a feeling of satisfaction, we can see how his character is bound up with his Sentient Soul, and how volitions connected with his higher soul-members come to expression hardly at all.

When, however, the activity of the Ego resonates in the Intellectual Soul, we can often observe a gesture related to the organ which serves the Intellectual Soul as its chief means of outer expression. Speakers who have the so-called "breast-tone of conviction" are given to striking themselves over the heart. They are men who speak with passion and are not concerned with objective judgment. Here we have the passionate character who lives entirely in the Sentient Soul but has so strong an Ego that his emotions resonate in the Intellectual Soul; we recognise him by his expansive attitudes. For example, there are popular speakers who thrust their thumbs into their waistcoats and swell out their chests when they are facing an audience. Far from being objective, they speak directly out of the Sentient Soul, putting into words their personal egoistic feelings and reinforcing them with this gesture—thumbs in waistcoat.

When the note struck by the Ego in the Sentient Soul resonates in the Consciousness Soul, we see a gesture bearing on the organ which gives the Consciousness Soul its chief outer expression. If a person finds it particularly difficult to bring his inner feelings to the point of reaching a decision, he will lay a finger on his nose—a gesture indicating how hard it is for him to fetch up a decision from the depth of his Consciousness Soul.

When someone lives chiefly in the Intellectual Soul, this is apparent in his physiognomy and facial expression. The experience of the Intellectual Soul lies closer to man's inner life and is not subject to the outer pressure under which he might sigh like a slave. He feels it to be more his own property, and this is reflected in his face. If a man is indeed capable of living in the Intellectual Soul, but presses down its content into the Sentient Soul, if any judgment he forms gets hold of him so strongly that he glows with enthusiasm for it, we can see this expressed in his sloping forhead and projecting chin. If something is actually experienced in the Intellectual Soul and only resonates in the Sentient Soul, this is expressed in the lower part of the face. If a man achieves

Human Character

the special virtue of the Intellectual Soul, a harmony between inner and outer, so that he neither secludes himself in inward brooding nor depletes his inner life by complete surrender to outer impressions, and if his Ego's work in the shaping of character is accomplished chiefly through the Intellectual Soul, then all this will be manifest in the middle part of his face, the external expression of the Intellectual Soul.

Here we can see how fruitful Spiritual Science can be for the study of civilisations: we are shown how successive characteristics are imprinted on successive peoples. Thus the Intellectual Soul made its imprint particularly on the ancient Greeks, among whom we can discern the beautiful harmony between inner and outer that is the characteristic manifestation of the Intellectual Soul. And here, accordingly, we find the Greek nose in its perfection. True it is that we cannot fully understand these things unless we relate them to their spiritual background.

Again, when someone carries the content of the Intellectual Soul into the realm of cognition and experiences it in the Consciousness Soul, the outward sign of this is a projecting forehead, as though the working of the Ego in the Intellectual Soul were flowing up into the Consciousness Soul.

If, however, someone lives in close unity with his Ego, so that the character of the Ego is impressed on the Consciousness Soul, he can then carry the note sounded by the Ego in his Consciousness Soul down into his Intellectual Soul and his Sentient Soul. This goes with a higher stage of human development. Only the Consciousness Soul can be permeated by high moral and aesthetic ideals and by great, wide-ranging conceptions of the world.

All this has to come to life in the Consciousness Soul, but the forces engendered by the Ego in the Consciousness Soul on this account can penetrate down into the Sentient Soul, where they are fired with enthusiasm and passion and with what we may call the inner warmth of the Sentient Soul. This comes about when a man can glow with enthusiasm for some knowledge he has gained. Then the noblest aspiration to which man can rise at present is carried down into the Sentient Soul. And the Sentient Soul itself is enhanced when permeated by forces from the Consciousness Soul. But what the Ego can accomplish for a character-ideal through its work in the Consciousness Soul may encounter obstacles caused by inborn predispositions, so that it cannot be impressed on the physical body. Then we have to practise resignation; the work of the Ego in the Consciousness Soul may give rise to a noble quality of soul, but this cannot come to expression in the physical body during that single life-time. But the ardent passion for high moral ideals that a person has experienced in the Sentient Soul can be taken through the gate of death and carried over into his next life as a most powerful formative force. We can see how this comes to expression in the contours of the skull, showing that what a man has made of himself penetrates into his very bones.

A study of the contours of the skull can indeed throw some light on character, but always in a strictly individual context. It is absurd to suppose that phrenology can lay down general schemes and typical principles that will be universally valid. Everyone has a phrenology that applies to himself alone, for his skull is shaped by forces derived from his previous life, and in every individual this must be recognised. Only abstract theorists addicted to diagrams would think of founding a phrenology on general principles. Anyone who knows about the formative forces that work into man's very bones would speak only of recognising their effects in individuals. The formation of the skull is different with everyone and can never be accounted for in terms of a single earthly life. Here we touch on what is called reincarnation, for in the contours of the skull we can discern what a man has made of himself in previous lives. Here reincarnation becomes a palpable fact. We need only know where to read the evidence for it.

Thus we see how the effects of human character have to be followed from their origin all the way into the hardest structures, and then human character stands before us as a wonderful riddle. We have begun to describe how the Ego impresses character into the forms of the Sentient Soul, the Intellectual Soul and the Consciousness Soul. Then we saw how this work by the Ego has results which make their mark on man's external physique and are manifest in gesture and physiognomy and even in the bones. And since man is led from birth to death and on again to a new birth, we saw how his inner being works on the outer, impressing character both on the inner life and on the physical body, which is an image of the inner life. Hence we can very well understand the deep impression made on us by the Laocoon, where we see the bodily character falling asunder into the several limbs; we see, as it were, the character, which belongs to the very essence of man, vanishing in the outward gestures of this work of art. Here we have plain evidence of the working of inner forces in the material realm, and of how the dispositions brought from earlier lives are determining factors in any given life; and we see how the spirit, by breaking life asunder, brings to expression in a new life the character acquired as the outcome of a previous one.

We can now enter into Goethe's feelings when he held Schiller's skull in his hand and said: In the contours of this skull I see how the the spirit sets its stamp on matter. This form, full of character, calls up

Human Character

for me the voice that I heard sounding through Schiller's poems and in the words of friendship he so often spoke to me. Yes, I see here how the spirit has worked in the material realm. And when I contemplate this piece of matter, its noble forms show me how previous lives prepared the radiance that shone out so powerfully for me from Schiller's mind.

So we are led to repeat as our own conviction the words written by Goethe after contemplating Schiller's skull:

> What greater gift can life on man bestow
> Than that to him God-Nature should disclose
> How solid to spirit it attenuates,
> How spirit's work it hardens and preserves.

LECTURE 6
Asceticism and Illness

Berlin, 11th November, 1909

Human life swings between work and idleness. The activity we are to discuss today, known as asceticism, is regarded either as work or as idleness according to the preconceptions of one person or another. An objective, unbiased study, such as Spiritual Science demands, is impossible unless we observe how what is called asceticism—in the highest sense excluding misuse of the word—influences human life, and either helps or harms it.

It is quite natural that most people today should have a somewhat false idea of what the word asceticism ought to mean. In its original Greek form it could apply as well to an athlete as to an ascetic. But in our time the word has acquired a particular colouring from the form taken by this way of life during the Middle Ages; and for many people the word has the flavour that Schopenhauer gave it in the 19th century.[35] Today the word is again acquiring a certain colouring through the manifold influences of oriental philosophy and religion, particularly through what the West usually calls Buddhism. Our task in this lecture is to find the true origin in human nature of asceticism; and Spiritual Science, as characterised in previous lectures, is called upon to bring clarity into this discussion, the more so because its own outlook is connected with the original meaning of the Greek word, *askesis*.

Spiritual Science and spiritual research, as they have been represented here for some years, take a quite definite attitude towards human nature. They start from the postulate that at no stage in the evolution of mankind is it justifiable to say that here or there are the limits of human knowledge. The usual way of putting the question, "What can man know, and what can he not know?", is for Spiritual Science misdirected. It does not ask what man can know at a certain stage in his evolution; or what the boundaries of knowledge are at that stage; or what remains hidden because at that time human cognition cannot penetrate it. All these matters are not its immediate concern; for Spiritual Science takes its stand on the firm ground of evolution, in particular the evolution of human soul-forces. It says that the human soul can develop. As in the seed of a plant the future plant sleeps and is called forth by the forces within the seed and those which work on it from without, so are hidden forces and capacities always sleeping in the human soul. What we cannot know at one stage of development we may know later, when we have advanced a little in developing our spiritual faculties.

Which are the forces that we can develop in ourselves for a deeper understanding of the world and the attainment of an ever wider horizon? That is the question asked by Spiritual Science. It does not ask where the boundaries of our knowledge are, but how man can surpass the bounds that exist at any given period by developing his capacities. Not through vague talk, but in a quite definite way, it shows how man can surpass the cognitive faculties that have been bestowed on him by an evolutionary process in which his own consciousness has not participated. In the first instance, these faculties are concerned only with the world perceived by our senses and grasped by our reason. But by means of the forces latent in the soul, man is able to penetrate into the worlds which are at first not open to the senses and cannot be reached by a reason bound up with the senses. In order that we may from the beginning avoid the charge of vagueness, I will describe quite briefly what you will find given fully in *Knowledge of the Higher Worlds: How is it Achieved?*

When we speak of passing beyond the ordinary bounds of knowledge, we must take care not to wander off into the blue, but rather find our way from the solid ground under our feet into a new world. How is it to be done?

In the normal human being of today, we have an alternation of the two conditions called "waking" and "sleeping".[36] Without going into details, we may say that for ordinary knowledge the difference lies in this, that while man is awake, his senses and the sense-bound intellect are under constant stimulus. It is this stimulus which wakens his external cognition, and during waking hours he is given up to the external sense-world. In sleep we are removed from that world. A simple logical consideration shows that it is not irrational for Spiritual Science to maintain that there is something in human nature which separates itself during sleep from what we usually call the human body. We know that for Spiritual Science the physical body, which can be seen with the eyes and touched with the hand, is only part of man. He has a second part, the so-called etheric or life-body. When we are asleep, the physical and etheric bodies remain in bed, and we separate from them what we call the consciousness body or—don't be put off by the terminology—the astral body, the bearer of desire and pain, pleasure and sorrow, of impulse and passion. In addition we have a fourth part, one which makes man the crown of earthly creation: the ego. These last two parts split off during sleep from the physical and the etheric bodies. A simple consideration, as I said, can teach us that it is not irrational for Spiritual Science to declare that what we have as pleasure and pain, or as the ego's power of judgment, cannot vanish during the night and be reborn anew every morning, but must remain in existence. Think, if you will, of this withdrawal of the astral body and the ego as a mere picture; in any case it is undeniable that the ego and the astral body withdraw from what we call the physical and the etheric bodies.

Now the peculiar thing is that these inmost parts of the human being, the astral body and the ego, within which we live through what we call soul-experience, sink down during sleep into an indefinite obscurity. But this means simply that this inmost part of the human being needs the stimulus of the external world if it is to be conscious of itself and of the external world. Hence we can say that at the moment of falling asleep, when this stimulus ceases, man cannot develop consciousness in himself. But if, in the normal course of his existence, a human being were able so to stimulate the inner parts of his being, so to fill them with energy and inner life, that he had a consciousness of them even when there were no sense-impressions and the sense-bound intellect was inactive and free from the stimulus of the external world, he would then be able to perceive other things than those which come through the stimulus of the senses. However strange and paradoxical it may sound, it is true that if a man could reproduce a condition which on the one hand resembles sleep, and yet is essentially different from it on the other, he could reach supersensible knowledge. His condition would resemble sleep in not depending on any external stimulus; the difference would be that he would not sink into unconsciousness but would unfold a vivid inner life.

As may be shown from spiritual-scientific experience, man can come to such a condition: a condition of clairvoyance, if the word is not misused, as it so often is today. I will give you briefly one example of the numerous inner exercises through which this condition can be attained.

If we wish to experience this condition safely, we must always start from the external world. The external world gives us mental images, and we call them true if we find that they correspond with external facts. But this kind of truth cannot raise us above external

Asceticism and Illness

reality. Our task, therefore, is to bridge the gulf between external perception and a perception which is independent of the senses and yet can give us truth. One of the first stages towards this form of knowledge is concerned with pictorial or symbolic concepts. As an example, let us take a symbol which is of use for spiritual development, and expound it in the form of a conversation between a teacher and his pupil.

In order to make his pupil understand this kind of symbolic picture,[37] the teacher might speak as follows: "Think of the plant, how it is rooted in the earth and grows from it, sends forth green leaf after green leaf and develops to flower and fruit." (We are not here concerned with ordinary scientific ideas, for, as we shall see, we are not discussing the essential difference between man and plant, but trying to get hold of a useful pictorial idea). The teacher may continue: "And now look at man. He certainly has a great deal that is not present in the plant. He can experience impulses, desires, emotions, a whole range of concepts which can lead him up the ladder from blind sensation and instinct to the highest moral ideals. Only a scientific fantasy could attribute similar consciousness to plants and to men; but on a lower level a plant has certain advantages. It has certainty of growth, without possibility of error, while man can deviate at any moment from his right place in the world. We can see how in his whole structure he is permeated with instincts, desires and passions which may bring him into error, delusion and falsehood. In contrast, the plant is in substance untouched by these things; it is a pure, chaste being. Only when man has purified his whole life of instinct and desire can he hope to be as pure on his higher level as the plant is in its certainty and security on the lower level."

Then we can pass to a further picture. The plant is permeated with the green colouring matter, chlorophyll, which steeps the leaves in green colour. Man is permeated with the vehicle of instincts and emotions, his red blood. That is a sort of evolution upwards, and in its course man has had to accept characteristics not found in the plant. He must hold before his eyes the high ideal of one day attaining on his own level to the inner purity, certainty and self-control of which we have a picture at a lower level in the plant. So we may ask what we must do in order to rise to that level.

Man must become lord and master of the instincts, passions and cravings which surge around, unsought, within him. He must grow beyond himself, kill within him all that normally dominates him, and raise to a higher level all that is dominated by the lower. This is how man has developed from the plant, and all that has been added since the plant stage he must look on as something to be conquered, in order to derive from it a higher life. That is the proper direction of man's future,

Metamorphoses of the Soul

indicated by Goethe in the fine stanza:

> Whoever cannot say
> Die and renew thyself!
> On our dark earth will be
> A mournful guest![38]

This does not mean that man must kill his instincts and emotions, but that he cleanses and purifies them by removing their mastery over him. So, in looking at the plant, he can say: "Something in me is higher than the plant, but I have to conquer and destroy it."

As a picture of what we have to overcome in ourselves, let us take that part of the plant which is no longer capable of life, the dry wood, and set it up in the form of a cross. The next task is to cleanse and purify the red blood, the vehicle of our instincts, impulses and cravings, so that it may be a pure, chaste expression of our higher being, of what Schiller meant when he spoke of "the higher man in man". The blood will then be, as it were, a copy in man of the pure sap which flows through the plant.

"Now"—the teacher will resume—"let us look at a flower in which the sap, rising up continuously, stage by stage, through the leaves, finally merges into the colour of the flower, the red rose. Picture the red rose as an image of your blood when your blood has been cleansed and purified. The sap of the plant pulses through the red rose and leaves it without impulses or desires; but your impulses and desires must come to be the expression of your purified ego." Thus we supplement our picture of the wood of the cross, which symbolises what we have to overcome, by hanging a garland of red roses upon the cross. Then we have a picture, a symbol, which does not appeal only to dry reasoning, but by stirring our feelings gives us an image of human life raised to the level of a higher ideal.

Someone may now say: Your picture is an invention which corresponds to nothing true. All that you conjure up, the black cross and the red rose is mere fancy. Yes, undoubtedly, this picture, as brought before the inner eye of anyone who wishes to rise into spiritual worlds, is an invention. That is just what it has to be! Its purpose is not to portray something that exists in the external world. If that were its function, we would not need it. We would be satisfied with the impressions of the outer world that come to us directly through our sense-perceptions. But the picture we create, though its elements are drawn from the external world, is based on certain feelings and ideas that belong to our own inner being. The essential thing is that we should be

Asceticism and Illness

fully conscious of each step, so that we keep a firm hold on the threads of our inner processes; otherwise we should be lost in illusion.

Anyone who wants to rise to higher worlds through inner meditation and contemplation does not live only in abstract pictures, but in a world of concepts and feelings which flow from these pictures he creates. The pictures call forth a number of activities in his soul, and by excluding every external stimulus he concentrates all his powers on contemplating the pictures. They are not meant to reflect external circumstances, but to awaken forces that slumber within him. If he is patient and perseveres—for progress comes slowly—he will notice that quiet devotion to pictures of this kind will give him something that can be further developed. He will soon find that his inner life is changing: a condition emerges that is in some respects akin to sleep. But while sleep brings a submergence of conscious soul-life, the devotion I have mentioned, and meditation on the symbolic pictures, cause inner forces to awaken. Very soon he feels that a change is going on within him, although he has excluded all impressions of the outer world. So through these quite unrealistic symbols he awakens inner forces, and he soon realises that he can put them to good use.

Someone may object again by saying: "That is all very well, but even if we develop these forces and really penetrate into the spiritual world, how can we be sure that what we perceive is reality?" Nothing can prove this except experience, just as the external world can be proved to exist only by experience. Mere concepts can be very strictly distinguished from perceptions and the two categories will be confused only be someone who has lost touch with reality. Especially in philosophical circles today, a certain misunderstanding has been gaining ground. Schopenhauer, [39] for instance, in the first part of his philosophy starts with the assumption that the world of man is a concept. Now you can see the difference between a percept and a concept by looking at your watch. As long as you are in contact with your watch, that is percept; if you turn round, you have a picture of the watch in your mind; that is concept. In practical life we very soon learn to distinguish between percept and concept, or we should go badly astray. If you picture a red-hot iron, however hot it is, you will not be burnt, but if you touch it you will soon realise that a percept is something other than a concept.

It is the same with an example given by Kant;[40] from a certain point of view it is justified, but during the last century it has been the source of much error. Kant tried to upset a certain concept of God by showing that there is no difference in content between the idea of a hundred shillings and a hundred real shillings. It is wrong, however, to maintain that there is no difference in the content, for then it is easy to confuse a perception, which gives us direct contact with reality, with the content of a mere concept. Anyone who has to pay a debt of a hundred shillings will soon find out the difference.

It is the same with the spiritual world. When we awaken the forces and faculties which are latent within us, and when around us is a world we have not known before, a world which shines out as though from a dark spiritual depth, then someone who enters this realm uninitiated might well say that it is all illusion and auto-suggestion. But anyone who has had real experiences on this level will be well able to distinguish reality from fantasy, just as in ordinary life we can distinguish between an imaginary piece of hot steel and a real one.

Thus we can see that it is possible to call forth a different form of consciousness. I have given you only one brief example of how inner exercises can work on the sleeping faculties of the soul. Of course, while we are still practising the exercises, we do not see a spiritual world; we are occupied in awakening the faculties required. In some circumstances this may last not merely for years, but for a whole life or lives. In the end, however, the result of these exercises is that the sleeping forces of cognition are awakened and directed towards a spiritual world, just as we have learnt to adapt the eye with the help of unknown spiritual powers to observing the external world. This work on one's own soul, this development of the soul to the stage of perceiving a world in which we are not yet living but to which we gain access through what we bring to it—this training can be called *asceticism* in the true sense of the word. For in Greek the word means working on oneself, making oneself capable of accomplishing something, transforming sleeping forces into active ones. This original meaning of the word can still be its meaning today if we refuse to be led astray by the false use of the term which has become common down the centuries. We shall understand the true meaning of asceticism as described here, only if we remember that the purpose of this working on oneself is to develop faculties which will open up a new world.

Now, having discussed asceticism in relation to the spiritual world only, it will be helpful to see how the term applies to certain activities in the external world. There it can signify the training of certain forces and capabilities which are not going to be used immediately for their final purpose, but are first to be exercised and made ready for it. An example close at hand will illustrate this, and will also show how an incorrect use of the term can have harmful results. The term can be rightly applied to military manoeuvres; this is quite in keeping with the original Greek usage. The deployment and testing of military forces

Asceticism and Illness

on these occasions, so that in real war they may be ready and available in the right numbers—that is ascetiscism exercise. Whenever forces are not used for their final purpose, but are tested in advance for efficiency and reliability, we have asceticism. Manoeuvres bear the same relation to warfare as asceticism does to life in general.

Human life, I said earlier, swings between work and idleness. But there are all sorts of intermediate stages: for example, play. Play, when it really is play, is the opposite of asceticism. And from its opposite one can see very well what asceticism is. Play is the active use of energies in the outer world for the sake of immediate gratification. The material of play is not, so to speak, the hard, unyielding substance of the external world that we encounter during hours of work. In relation to our energies it is malleable, amenable to our exertions. Play is play only when we do not knock up against the resistance of outer forces, as we do in work. Play is concerned with a direct release of energies which are transformed into achievement, and therein lies the satisfaction we get from it. Play does not prepare us for anything; it finds fulfilment in and through itself.

It is just the opposite with asceticism, if we take the term in its proper sense. In this case no gratification is gained from anything in the outer world. Whenever we combine things in asceticism, if only the cross and the red roses, the combination is not significant in itself, but only in so far as it calls our inner forces into activity, an activity which will find application only when it has ripened fully within ourselves. Renunciation comes in because we work inwardly on ourselves while knowing that at first we are not to be stimulated by the outer world. Our aim is to bring into activity our inner forces, so that they may be applied to the outer world later on. Play and asceticism, accordingly, are opposites.

How does asceticism, in our sense of the word, enter practically into human life? Let us keep to a sphere where asceticism can be practised both in a right and in a wrong way. We will take the case of someone who makes it his aim to ascend into spiritual worlds. If, then, a supersensible world comes by some means or other to his attention, whether through another person or through some historical document, he may say: There are statements and communications concerning the supersensible worlds, but at present they are beyond my comprehension; I lack the power to understand them. Then there are others who reject these communications, refuse to have anything to do with them. What is the source of this attitude? It arises because a person of this type rejects asceticism in the best sense of the word; he cannot find in his soul the strength to use the means I have described

Metamorphoses of the Soul

for developing higher faculties. He feels too weak for it.

I have repeatedly emphasised that clairvoyance is not necessary for understanding the findings of clairvoyant research. Clairvoyance is indeed necessary for gaining access to spiritual facts, but once the facts have been communicated, anyone can use unprejudiced reason to understand them. Impartial reason and healthy intellect are the best instruments for judging anything communicated from the spiritual worlds. A true spiritual scientist will always say that if he could be afraid of anything, he would be afraid of people who accept communications of this kind without testing them strictly by means of reason. He is never afraid of those who make use of unclouded intelligence, for that is what makes all these communications comprehensible.

However, a man may feel too weak to call forth in himself the forces necessary for understanding what he is told concerning the spiritual world. In that case he turns away from all this through an instinct for self-preservation which is right for him. He feels that to accept these communications would throw his mind into confusion. And in all cases where people reject what they hear through Spiritual Science, an instinct of self-preservation is at work; they know that they are incapable of doing the necessary exercises—that is, of practising asceticism in the true sense. A person prompted by the instinct for self-preservation will then say to himself: If these things were to permeate my spiritual life, they would confuse it; I could make nothing of them and therefore I reject them. So it is with a materialistic outlook which refuses to go a step beyond the doctrines of a science it believes to be firmly founded on facts. But there are other possibilities, and here we come to a dangerous side of asceticism. People may have a sort of avidity for information about the spiritual world while lacking the inner urge and conscience to test everything by reason and logic. They may indulge a liking for sensationalism in this field. Then they are not held back by an instinct for self-preservation, but are driven on by its very opposite, a sort of urge for self-annihilation. If anyone takes something into his soul without understanding it, and with no wish to apply his reason to it, he will be swamped by it. This happens in all cases of blind faith, or when communications from the spiritual worlds are accepted merely on authority. This acceptance corresponds to an asceticism which derives not from a healthy instinct for self-preservation, but from a morbid impulse to annihilate the self, to drown in a flood of revelations. This has a significant shadow-side in the human soul: it is a bad form of asceticism when someone gives up all effort and chooses to live in faith and in reliance on others.

This attitude has existed in many forms in many epochs. But we

Asceticism and Illness

must not assume that everything which looks like blind faith is so. For example, we are told that in the old Pythagorean Mystery Schools[41] there was a familiar phrase: The Master has said. But this never meant: The Master has said, therefore we believe it! For his students it meant something like this: The Master has said; therefore it demands that we should reflect on it and see how far we can get with it if we bring all our forces to bear upon it. To "believe" need not always imply a blind belief springing from a desire for self-annihilation. It need not be blind belief if you accept communications springing from spiritual research because you trust the researcher. You may have learnt that his statements are in strictly logical form, and that in other realms, where his utterances can be tested, he is logical and does not talk nonsense. On this verifiable ground the student can hold a well-founded belief that the speaker, when he is talking about things not yet known to the student, has an equally sure basis for his statements. Hence the student can say: I will work! I have confidence in what I have been told, and this can be a guiding star for my endeavours to raise myself to the level of the faculties which will make themselves intelligible of their own accord, when I have worked my way up to them.

If this healthy foundation of trust is lacking and a person allows himself to be stirred by communications from the invisible worlds without understanding them, he will drift into a very wretched condition that is not compatible with asceticism. Whenever a person accepts something in blind faith without resolving to work his way to an understanding of it, and if therefore he accepts another person's will instead of his own, he will gradually lose those healthy soul-forces which provide the inner life with a sure centre and endow us with a true feeling for what is right. Lies and a proneness to error will beset a person who is unwilling to test inwardly, with his reason, what he is told; he will tend to drown and to lose himself in it. Anyone who does not allow himself to be guided by a healthy sense of truth will soon find how prone he is to lies and deceptions even in the outer world. When we approach the spiritual world we need to reflect very seriously that through this surrender of our judgment we can very easily fall into a life which no longer has any real feeling for truth and reality. If we seriously practise the exercises and wish to train our inner powers, we must never give up bringing before our souls the kind of knowledge I have been describing.

We can now penetrate further into what may be called the ascetic training of the soul in a deeper sense. So far we have considered only people who are not capable of developing these inner forces in a healthy way. In one case a sound instinct of self-preservation made a person

Metamorphoses of the Soul
refuse to develop these forces because he did not want to develop them; in the other case a person did not absolutely refuse to develop them, but he refused to bring his judgment and intelligence to bear on them. In all such cases the impulse is always to remain on the old level, at the old standpoint. But let us suppose a case where a person really does try to develop these inner faculties, and makes use of such forms of training as those we have described. Again there may be a dual result. It may be the result we always aim at, where Spiritual Science is taken seriously and worthily. A person will then be guided to develop his inner forces only in so far as he is capable of using them in a right and orderly way. Here, then, we are concerned with how a person has to work on himself —as is described in greater detail in my book, *Knowledge of the Higher Worlds: How is it Achieved?*—in order to awaken the faculties which will open the spiritual world to his inner sight. But at the same time he must be competent to discipline his faculties and to establish the right balance between his work on himself and his dealings with the outer world. The necessity of this has been proved by spiritual researchers down the ages.

If a person fails to apply his inner forces properly to his handling of the outer world and gives way to an almost uncontrollable urge to develop his soul-powers more and more to bring about all possible movement in his soul, so that he may thereby open his spirit-eyes and spirit-ears; and if he is too indolent to absorb slowly and in the right way the available facts of Spiritual Science and to work on them with his reason, then his asceticism may do him great harm. A person can develop all sorts of faculties and powers and yet not know what to do with them or how to apply them to the outer world. This, indeed, is the outcome of many forms of training and it applies to those who fail to pursue energetically the methods we have described, whereby the student is continually strengthening himself.

There are other methods with a different aim: they may be more comfortable but they can easily cause harm. Such methods aim at doing away with the hindrances imposed on the soul by the bodily nature, in order to enhance the inner life. This was in fact the sole endeavour of mediaeval ascetics, and it survives in part today. Instead of true asceticism, which sets out to give the soul an ever-richer content, false asceticism leaves the soul as it is and sets out to weaken the body and to reduce the activity of its forces. There are indeed ways of damping down these forces, so that the functioning of the body gradually weakens, and the result may then be that the soul, though itself remaining weak, gets the upper hand over the weakened body. A correct asceticism leaves the body as it is and enables the soul to master it; the other

Asceticism and Illness

asceticism leaves the soul as it is, while all sorts of procedures, fasting, mortifications and so on, are used to weaken the body. The soul is then relatively the stronger and can achieve a kind of consciousness, although its own powers have not increased. That is the way of many ascetics in the Middle Ages: they kill the vigour of the body, lower its activities, leave the soul as it is, and then live in the expectation that the content of the spiritual world will be revealed to them with no contribution on their part.

That is the easier method, but it is not a truly strengthening one. The true method requires a person to cleanse and purify his thinking, feeling and willing, so that these faculties will be strengthened and able to prevail over the body. The other method lowers the tone of the body, and the soul is then supposed to wait, without having acquired any new capacities, until the divine world flows into it.

You will find plenty of references to this method under the heading of "asceticism" in the Middle Ages. It leads to estrangement from the world and is bound to do so. For at the present stage of human evolution there is a certain relationship between our capabilities of perception and the outer world, and if we are to rise above this stage we can do so only by heightening our capabilities and using them to understand the outer world in its deeper significance. But if we weaken our normal forces, we make ourselves incapable of maintaining a normal relationship with the outer world; and especially if we tone down our thinking, feeling and willing and give our souls over to passive expectation, something will then flow into our souls which has no connection with our present-day world, makes us strangers there, and is useless for working in the world. While the true asceticism makes us more and more capable in our dealings with the world, for we see more and more deeply into it, the other asceticism, associated with the suppression of bodily functions, draws a person out of the world, tends to make him a hermit, a mere settler there. In this isolation he may see all sorts of psychic and spiritual things—this must not be denied—but an asceticism of this kind is of no use for the world. True asceticism is work, training for the world, not a withdrawal of oneself into remoteness from the world.

This does not imply that we have to go to the opposite extreme; there can be accommodation on both sides. Even though it is true in general that for our period in human evolution a certain normal relationship exists between the external world and the forces of the soul, yet every period tends to drive the normal to extremes as it were, and if we want to develop higher faculties we need pay no attention to opposition that comes from abnormal trends. And because we find the opposition

Metamorphoses of the Soul

in ourselves, we can under certain circumstances go rather further than would be necessary if the times were not also at fault.

I say this because you have perhaps heard that many followers of Spiritual Science lay great stress on a certain diet. This does not at all imply that such a mode of life can do anything for the attainment or even the understanding of higher worlds and higher relationships. It can be no more than an external aid, and should be seen only in relation to the fact that anyone wishing to gain understanding of the higher worlds may find a certain obstacle in the customs and conventions he has to live with at the present day. Because these conventions have drawn us down too deeply into the material world, we must go beyond the normal in order to make the exercises easier. But it would be quite mistaken to regard this as a form of asceticism which can be a means of leading us to higher worlds. Vegetarianism will never lead anyone to higher worlds; it can be no more than a support for someone who thinks to himself: I wish to open for myself certain ways of understanding the spiritual worlds; I am hindered by the heaviness of my body, which prevents the exercises from having an immediate effect. Hence I will make things easier by lightening my body. Vegetarianism is one way of producing this result, but it should never be presented as a dogma; it is only a means which can help some people to gain understanding of the spiritual worlds. No-one should suppose that a vegetarian way of life will enable him to develop spiritual powers. For it leaves the soul as it is and serves only to weaken the body. But if the soul is strengthened, it will be able though the effects of vegetarianism to strengthen the weakened body from the centre of its own forces. Anyone who develops spiritually with the aid of vegetarianism will be stronger, more efficient and more resistant in daily life; he will be not merely a match for any meat-eater but will be superior in working capacity. That is the very opposite of what is believed by many people when they say of vegetarians within a spiritual movement: How sad for these poor folk who can never enjoy a little bit of meat!

So long as a person has this feeling about vegetarianism, it will not bring him the slightest benefit. So long as a desire for meat persists, vegetarianism is useless. It is helpful only when it results from an attitude that I will illustrate with a little story.

Not very long ago, someone was asked: "Why don't you eat meat?" He replied with a counter-question: "Why don't you eat dogs or cats?" "One just can't", was the answer. "Why can't you?" "Because I would find it disgusting." "Well, that is just what I feel about all meat."

That is the point. When pleasure in eating meat has gone, then to abstain from meat may be of some use in relation to the spiritual worlds.

Asceticism and Illness

Until then, breaking the meat-eating habit can be helpful only for getting rid of the desire for meat. If the desire persists, it may be better to start eating meat again, for to go on tormenting oneself about it is certainly not the right way to reach an understanding of Spiritual Science.

From all this you can see the difference between true and false asceticism. False asceticism often attracts people whose sole desire is to develop the inner forces and faculties of the soul; they are indifferent towards gaining real knowledge of the outer world. Their aim is simply to develop their inner faculties and then to wait and see what comes of it. The best way of doing this is to mortify the body as far as possible, for this weakens it, and then the soul, though itself remaining weak, can see into some kind of spiritual world, however incapable it may be of understanding the real spiritual world. This, however, is a path of deception, for directly a person closes off his means of return to the physical world, he encounters no true spiritual world, but only delusive pictures of his own self. And these are what he is bound to encounter as long as he leaves his soul as it is. Because his ego keeps to its accustomed standpoint, it does not rise to higher powers, and he puts up a barrier between himself and the world by suppressing the functions which relate him to the world. It is not only that this kind of asceticism estranges him from the world; he sees pictures which can deceive him as to the stage his soul has reached, and in place of a true spiritual world he sees a picture clouded over by his own self.

There is a further consequence which leads into the realm of morality. Anyone who believes that humility and surrender to the spiritual world will set him on the right course of life fails to see that he is involving himself most strongly in his own self and becoming an egoist in the worst sense, for it means that he is content with himself as he is and has no wish to progress any further. This egoism, which can degenerate into unrestrained ambition and vanity, is the more dangerous because the victim of it cannot see it for himself. Generally he looks on himself as a man who sinks down in deepest humility at the feet of his God, while really he is being played on by the devil of megalomania. A genuine humility would tell him something he refuses to recognise, for it would lead him to say to himself: The powers of the spiritual world are not to be found at the stage where I am standing now: I must climb up to them; I must not rest content with the powers I already have.

So we see the results of the false asceticism which relies primarily on killing off external things instead of strengthening the inner life: it conduces to deception, error, vanity and egotism. In our time, especially, it would be a great evil if this course were followed as a means of entering the spiritual world. It serves merely to engross man in himself. Today the only true asceticism must be sought in modern Spiritual Science, founded on the firm ground of reality. Through it a person can develop his own faculties and forces and thus rise to a comprehension of a spiritual world which is itself a real world, not one that a man spins round himself.

This false asceticism has yet another shadow-side. If you look at the realms of nature around us, leading up from plants through animals to man, you will find the vital functions changing in character stage by stage. For example, the diseases of plants come only from some external cause, from abnormal conditions of wind and weather, light and sunshine. These external circumstances can produce illness in plants. If we go on to consider animals, we find that they also, if left to themselves are greatly superior to human beings in their fund of natural health. A human being may fall ill not only through the life he leads or through external circumstances, but also as a result of his inner life. If his soul is not well suited to his body, if the spiritual heritage he brings from earlier incarnations cannot adapt itself completely to his bodily constitution, these inner causes may bring about illnesses which are very often wrongly diagnosed. They can be symptoms of a maladjustment between soul and body.

We often find that people with these symptoms are inclined to rise to higher worlds by killing off their bodily nature. This is because the illness itself induces them to separate their souls from bodies which the soul has not fully permeated. In such people the body hardens itself in the most varied ways and closes in on itself; and since they have not strengthened the soul, but have used its weakness in order to escape from the influence of the bodily nature, and have thus drawn away from the body the health-giving strengthening forces of the soul, the body is made susceptable to all sorts of ailments. While a true asceticism strengthens the soul, which then works back on the body and makes it resistant to illness coming from outside, a false asceticism makes a person vulnerable to any illness of that kind.

That is the dangerous connection between false asceticism and the illnesses of our time. And it is this that gives rise in wide circles, where such things are easily misunderstood, to manifold errors as to the influence a spiritual-scientific outlook can have on those who adopt it. For people who seek to come to a sight of the spiritual world by way of a false asceticism are a fearful spectacle for onlookers. Their false asceticism opens up a wide field of action for harmful influences from the outer world. For these people, far from being strengthened to

Asceticism and Illness

resist the errors of our time, are well and truly exposed to them. Examples of this can be seen in many theosophical tendencies today. Merely calling oneself a "Theosophist" does not automatically guarantee the ability to act as a spiritual impulse against the adverse currents of the present time. When materialism prevails in the world, it is to some extent in tune with the concepts which are formed in observing the sense-world. Hence we can say that the materialism which applies to the external world and knows nothing of a spiritual world is in a certain sense justified. But in the case of an outlook which sets out to impart something about the spiritual world and takes into itself a caricature of the materialistic prejudices of our day because it is not founded on a real strengthening of spiritual forces, the result is much worse. A theosophical outlook permeated by contemporary errors may in some circumstances be much more harmful than a materialistic outlook; and it should be remarked that thoroughly materialistic concepts have spread widely in theosophical circles. So we hear the spiritual spoken of not as *Spirit,* but as though the spirit were only an infinitely refined form of nebulous matter. In speaking of the etheric body, these people picture only the physical refined beyond a certain point, and then they speak of etheric "vibrations". On the astral level the vibrations are still finer; on the mental level they are finer still, and so on. "Vibrations" everywhere! Anyone who relies on these concepts will never attain to the spiritual world; he will remain embedded in the physical world to which these concepts ought to be confined.

In this way a materialistic haze can be thrown over the most ordinary occasions in daily life. For instance, if we are at a social gathering which has a pleasant atmosphere, with people in harmony, and someone remarks on it in those terms, that may be a humdrum way of putting it; but it is a true way and leads to a better understanding than if at a gathering of theosophists one of them says how good the vibrations are. To say that, one has to be a theosophical materialist with crude ideas. And for anyone with a feeling for such things, the whole atmosphere goes out of tune when these vibrations are said to be dancing around. In these cases one can see how the introduction of materialistic ideas into a spiritual outlook produces a horrifying impression on outsiders, who may then say: These people talk about a spiritual world, but they are really no different from us. With us, the light waves dance; with them the spiritual waves dance. It is all the same materialism.

All this needs to be seen in its true light. Then we shall not get a wrong idea of what the spiritual-scientific movement has to offer in our time. We shall see that asceticism, by strengthening the soul, can itself lead to the spiritual world and so bring new forces into our material existence. These are forces that make for health, not for illness; they carry healthy life-forces into our bodily organism. Of course it is not easy to determine how far a given outlook brings healthy or unhealthy forces with it, for the latter are strongly evident, as a rule, while healthy forces are usually not noticed. However, a close observer will see how persons who stand in the stream of true Spiritual Science are fertilised by it and draw from it health-giving forces which work right down into the physical. He will see also that signs of illness appear only if something alien to a spiritual stream is introduced into it. Then the result can be worse than when the alien influence takes its course in the outer world, where people are shielded by conventions from carrying certain errors to an extreme.

If we see things in this light, we shall understand true asceticism as a preparatory training for a higher life, a way of developing our inner forces; and we shall then be taking the good old Greek word in its right sense. For to practise asceticism means training oneself, making oneself strong, even "adorning" oneself (*sich schmücken*), so that the world can see what it means to be human. But if asceticism leads you to leave the soul as it is and to weaken the bodily organism, the effect is that the soul is sundered from the body; the body is then exposed to all sorts of harmful influences and the asceticism is actually the source of all manner of ailments.

The good and bad sides of egoism will emerge when we come to consider its nature. Today I have shown how true asceticism can never be an end in itself, but only a means of reaching a higher human goal, the conscious experiencing of higher worlds. Anyone wishing to practise this asceticism must therefore keep his feet firmly planted on solid ground. He must not be a stranger to the world in which he lives, but must always be extending his knowledge of the world. Whatever he can bring back from higher worlds must always be measured and assessed in relation to his work in the world; otherwise those who say that asceticism is not work but idleness could well be right. And idleness can easily give occasion for false asceticism, especially in our time. Anyone, however, who keeps a firm foothold on the earth, will regard asceticism as his highest ideal in relation to so serious a subject as our human faculties. Our ideas can indeed rise high if we have before us an ideal picture of how our faculties should work in the world.

Let us look for a moment at the opening of the Old Testament: "And God said, Let there be light." Then we hear how God caused the physical sense-world to arise day by day from the spiritual, and how at the end of each day God looked at his creation and "saw that it was good."

Asceticism and Illness

Similarly we must maintain our healthy thinking, our reliable character, our unerring feelings on the firm ground of reality, in order that we may rise to higher worlds and discover there the facts which give birth to the entire physical world. Then, when as searchers we come to know the spirit, and when we apply to the world around us the forces we have developed and see how well adapted to it they are, we can see that this is good. If we test the forces we have acquired through true asceticism by putting them to work in the world, then we have the right to say: Yes, they are good.

LECTURE 7
Human Egoism

Berlin, 25th November, 1909

Once upon a time a Society was founded with a programme announcing as its central aim: "The abolition of egoism". All its members had to pledge themselves to cultivate selflessness and freedom from egoism in any form. This Society had elected a President, as all societies do, and the thing now, was to gain support for its fundamental principle in the world at large.

It was emphatically laid down over and over again and in the most diverse ways that no member at any time or place (and especially within the Society) should cherish the slightest egoistic wish or give utterance to any kind of selfish desire.

Now this was certainly a Society with an uncommonly praiseworthy programme and an exalted human goal. But one could not immediately say that the members were seeking to exemplify in themselves the primary point in their programme, for they scarcely allowed themselves to become acquainted with unselfish human wishes. The following scene was often enacted within the Society. A member would say: "Yes, I would like this and that. But if I were to put it to the Chairman, I would be advancing an egoistic wish, and that would never do." Another member would reply: "Quite simple—I'll go on your behalf. I shall be acting as your representative, and in putting forward your wish I shall be doing something entirely selfless. But listen—there is something I would like. Naturally, it is something quite egoistic, so according to our programme I can't propose it." The first member would then say: "If you are to be so unselfish on my account, I will do something for you. I will go to the Chairman on your behalf and ask him for what you want." And so it turned out. One of the two went first to the Chairman and then, two hours later, the other member went. Both had put forward quite unselfish wishes.

Human Egoism

"Once upon a time", I said—of course this Society has never existed. But anyone who looks round him in daily life will perhaps agree that a little of this Society is always present everywhere. At all events, my intention was only to indicate how "egoism" is one of those words which most readily become catch-words unless they are used in a direct connection with whatever they designate; otherwise they appear in disguise and deceive us into passing casually over them.

Today we will take this catch-word, egoism, and its opposite, altruism or selflessness. We shall not treat them as catch-words, but will try to penetrate a little way into the nature of egoism. When we examine these things from the standpoint of Spiritual Science, we are not so much concerned with whatever sympathy or antipathy may be evoked by this or that human characteristic, or how it may be assessed in accordance with some prevailing judgment—these are not important points. What matters much more, is to show how the relevant characteristic originates in the human soul, and within what limits it is valid; and if it must be fought against, to determine how far it can be combatted through human nature or through other existent beings.

In its literal sense, egoism is the characteristic which impels a man to give first place to his own advantage and the enhancement of his own personality, while its opposite, altruism, aims at placing human faculties at the service of others, indeed, of the whole world.

A simple consideration will show us how precarious our position is if we think only of the word egoism, and fail to enter into the thing itself. Suppose that someone proves himself to be a great benefactor in one way or another. It could well be that he is a benefactor only out of egoism, perhaps out of quite petty forms of egoism, perhaps out of vanity and the like. On the other hand, if a man is dubbed an egoist without more ado, this is by no means the last word on his character. For if a man seeks only to satisfy himself but otherwise has noble qualities, so that he sees the service of others as the best way forward for himself, we might perhaps be well pleased with such an "egoist". This may sound like a mere play on words, but is more than that, for in fact this playing on words permeates our entire life and shows itself in all realms of existence.

For everything we find in man we can find something analagous in the rest of the world. Schiller has a verse which indicates how in the realms of Nature something symbolical of an outstanding human quality can be found:

> Seek you the highest, the greatest?
> The plant can teach it to you.

Metamorphoses of the Soul

> What the plant does without willing it,
> Go you and do by willing it.[42]

Schiller here brings before us the being of the plant and urges man to develop in his own character something as noble as the plant is on its own level. And the great German mystic, Angelus Silesius, says much the same:

> Not asking why or wherefore blooms the rose
> Cares not for herself or whether men behold her.[43]

Here again we are called to look at the plant world. The plant draws in whatever it needs for growth; it asks no why or wherefore; it flowers because it flowers and cares not whom it may concern. And yet, it is by drawing its life-forces and everything it needs for itself from its environment that the plant acquires whatever worth it can have for its environment and finally for men. Indeed, it attains the highest degree of usefulness that can be imagined for a created being, if it belongs to those realms of the plant world which can be of service to higher beings. And it will now be an idle triviality to repeat here a familiar saying, although it has been quoted so often:

> When herself the rose adorns,
> She adorns the garden.[44]

When the rose is as beautiful as it can be, the garden is adorned. We can connect this with the word, egoism, and say: When the rose strives quite egoistically to be as beautiful as she can, and to grace herself with the finest possible form, then through her the garden becomes as beautiful as possible. Can we take this result from a lower level of existence and apply it in some way to man? We have no need to do this, for it has been done already by many others, and by Goethe best of all.

When Goethe wishes to express what man is in the most authentic sense, and how he manifests most truly his worth and the entire content of his existence, he says: "When a man's healthy nature works as a whole, when he feels himself to be living in the world as in a great and beautiful and worthy whole, when this harmony brings him a pure, free joy, then the universe, if it could come to be aware of its own self, would cry out in exultation at having reached its goal and would marvel at the height which its own being and becoming had attained."

This passage is from Goethe's splendid book on Winckelmann,[45] and elsewhere in the same book he says: "Placed upon the summit

Human Egoism

of Nature, man sees himself as another complete nature, with the task of achieving another summit in himself. To this end he heightens his powers, imbuing himself with all perfections and virtues, invoking choice, order, harmony and meaning, and finally rising to the creation of a work of art.''

Goethe's whole mood shows that he is referring here to the artist only as a specialised example and that he really means: Placed upon the summit of Nature, man gathers together everything that the world can express in him and finally displays to the world its own image, mirrored from within himself; and Nature would rejoice if she could perceive in the human soul this reflected image of herself.

What else does this mean than that everything which surrounds us in the world, as Nature and as spirit, concentrates itself in man, rises to a summit, and becomes in individual men, in the individual human Ego, as beautiful, true and perfect as it can? Hence, man will best fulfil his existence if he draws in as much as possible from the outer world and makes his own everything that can blossom and bear fruit in himself.

This view of things implies that man can never do enough to combine in himself whatever the surrounding world offers, in order to manifest through himself a kind of supreme achievement of Nature. Anyone who wishes to call that "egoism" may do so. Then one could say: The human ego is there to be an organ for elements in Nature which would otherwise remain forever hidden and which can come to expression only through being concentrated in the spirit of man. But although it is natural for man to gather these elements from the natural world into himself, it also lies in his nature to bring error and confusion into the general law which leads the lower realms in outer existence towards the highest levels. This is bound up with what we call human freedom. Man could never enjoy a free existence if he were not capable of misusing in a one-sided way certain forces within him—forces which can lead to the heights and can also pervert existence and perhaps even make a caricature of it. A simple comparison will make this clear. Let us go back to the plant.

It does not generally occur to us to speak of egoism in connection with the plant. It was only in order to bring out clearly the law of egoism that we said: What comes to expression in the plants could be called egoism. Normally, we do not speak of egoism in their case. If we consider the plant world in a spiritual and not a materialistic sense, we can see that the plant is in a certain sense proof against egoism. On the one hand, the conditions of its life require it to make itself as beautiful as it can, without asking who will benefit from its beauty.

Metamorphoses of the Soul

But when the plant has risen to the highest expression of its individual being, it is on the verge of having to give all this up. The plant world has a peculiar characteristic. Goethe puts this finely in his Prose Sayings: "The law of vegetable growth reaches its highest manifestation in the blossom and of this, in him, the rose is the summit. . . The fruit can never be beautiful, for then the vegetable law retreats and becomes again merely a law."[46] Thus it was clear to Goethe that the plant gives expression to its own law most vividly when it flowers. At this moment, however, it must be prepared to yield up its beauty to the process of fructification, for it is now called upon to sacrifice its highest self on behalf of its successor in the form of the seed-bud. There is something great in this act of self-sacrifice by the plant at the moment when it is rising to the point of imprinting its Ego, as it were, on its appearance. So on this lower level, we see how in Nature egoism progresses to a certain stage, and how it then destroys and surrenders itself in order that something new may emerge. The highest manifestation of the plant, its individuality—as we may call it—which achieves its summit of beauty in the flower, begins to fade directly the new plant-seed is produced.

Now let us ask: Does anything similar occur on the human level? Yes, if we consider Nature and spiritual life in terms of the spirit, we find that something quite similar does occur in man. For man is not intended merely to reproduce his kind and to carry on the human species; he is called upon to transcend the species and to exist as an individual. We shall come to know the true form and nature of egoism in man only if we look at his being in the light of previous lectures.

In Spiritual Science, we do not regard man as consisting only of a physical body, which he has in common with the mineral kingdom. We speak of higher members of his being: the etheric body which he has in common with all living things, and the astral body, or consciousness body, the bearer of pleasure and pain, joy and sorrow, which he has in common with the animal kingdom. And we say, that within these three members lives the true kernel of his being, the Ego. We must regard the Ego as the bearer of egoism both when the latter is justified and when it is unjustified. Man's development depends entirely on the work accomplished by the Ego in transforming the other three members of his being. At first, on a primitive level, his Ego is the slave of these other members; he follows all the urges, desires and passions that come from his astral body. But the further his development goes, the more will he be doing to purify his astral body, so that he transforms it into something which is ruled by his higher nature, by his Ego, and his Ego becomes increasingly the ruler and purifier of the other members of his being.

Human Egoism

As you have heard in previous lectures, man is now in the midst of this development. In so far as he transforms his astral body, he creates what we call Spirit-self, or, in the terminology of oriental philosophy, Manas. In the future it will be possible for him to transform by degrees his etheric body, and so to create what we call Life-spirit, or Buddhi. And when finally he masters the processes in his physical body, the transformed part of it will be what we call Atman, or Spirit-man. So we look towards a future condition in which man will rule consciously, from out of his Ego, over all his activities.

These future faculties have been in preparation for a very long time. The Ego has already worked, unconsciously or subconsciously, on the three other members of man's being. In the far distant past the Ego transformed a part of the astral body, also called the sentient body, into the Sentient Soul; a part of the etheric body into the Intellectual Soul, and a part of the physical body into the Consciousness Soul. Today we shall be concerned especially with the relationship of the sentient body to the Sentient Soul.

When we observe a human being from the time of his birth and see how his faculties gradually emerge—as though from the hidden depths of his bodily nature, we can say: Here the Sentient Soul is working its way out into the light of day. The Sentient Soul, as we have seen, is fashioned by the Ego out of the sentient body, and the sentient body is built up from the young child's entire environment. We can understand this if we recall Goethe's saying: "The eye is formed by light for light."[47] If we consider any sense-organ whereby man becomes conscious of the external physical world, we must set against Schopenhauer's one-sided statement,[48] that we could not see the light if we had no eyes, the equally valid statement that if there were no light, there would be no eyes. Through endless ages, as Goethe says, the all-pervading light worked on the human organism so as to fashion the sense-organ which is now able to look on the light. We can discern in the world around us the forces which have produced in man the faculties which enable us to become conscious of it. Thus the entire sentient body, the whole fabric whereby we enter into a relationship with the outer world, has been woven from its living forces. We have no share in this achievement. The astral body is a product, a flowering, of the surrounding world. Within the astral body the Sentient Soul emerges, formed by the work of the Ego from the substance of the sentient body. So the Ego lives in the sentient body and draws from it the substance of the Sentient Soul.

Now the Ego can work in a twofold way. First, it can develop in the Sentient Soul those faculties which are in harmony with the faculties

Metamorphoses of the Soul

and characteristics of the sentient body. An example from the field of education will make this clear. It is precisely from the field of education that we can draw the most beautiful and practical examples of what Spiritual Science is.

The sentient body is built up from a child's environment. Hence all those concerned with bringing up and educating a child have an influence on the sentient body, from the very beginning of its physical existence. They can help the sentient body to acquire the soul-qualities that are in harmony with its characteristics, as indicated by the Ego; but they can also pass on things which contradict these characteristics. If a child is brought up and educated in such a way that he can feel a living interest in everything that meets his eyes, if he can rightly rejoice in colours and forms, if musical tones give him happiness, if he can gradually bring about harmony between the impressions that come to him from outside and the feelings of joy and pleasure, of sympathetic interest in life, that arise in the Sentient Soul—then the child's inner response will be in consonance with a true picture of existence; then the inner life of his soul will harmonise with outer existence. Then, secondly, we can say that a human being does not live only within himself, capable only of fashioning a Sentient Soul in his sentient body; he can go out beyond himself. Nor is he capable only of seeing and hearing; he can pour himself out into the surrounding world and live in whatever his sentient body transmits to him. Then we have not only harmony between sentient body and Sentient Soul; we have harmony also between the outer world and the experiences of the Sentient Soul. Then man is truly a kind of mirror of the universe; a kind of microcosm which—as Goethe said—enjoys the feeling of living in the wide expanse of a great and beautiful world.

We can take another example. If a child were to grow up on a desert island, far from any human society, some of its faculties would not develop. It would be deprived of speech, of thinking power, and of all those noble qualities which can light up only through living together with other human beings, for these are qualities which belong to man's inner being, to his soul.

Now man can develop in such a way that he goes out from himself, with his attributes, and creates harmony between himself and the world around him. Or he can let his endowments harden and dry up within himself. This happens if he fails to respond to the colours, tones and so on that he receives from the outer world, and so is unable to give them back enriched with his own interest and pleasure. A man becomes inwardly hardened if he keeps to himself whatever he acquires from associating with other people, instead of making it contribute to human

Human Egoism

intercourse. If he secludes himself, choosing to live entirely within himself, a disharmony arises between him and his environment. A cleft opens between his Sentient Soul and his sentient body. If, after enjoying the advantages of human progress, he fails to place at the service of mankind the benefits that can flourish only in a social milieu, a gap arises between himself and his surroundings, whether it be the outer world, to which he can no longer respond, or his human environment, to which he owes his finest interests. The result is that he becomes inwardly dried up, for he cannot be advanced or enlivened by anything that comes to him from outside if it is torn from its roots, and this is what happens if he fails to allow his soul-life to flow out into the world around him. And if he continually reinforces his seclusion from the outer world, the effect is that his soul-life tends to wither and die away. This is precisely the bad side of egoism, and we must now characterise it in greater detail.

When egoism takes this form, so that man is not continually nourished and vitalised by the outer world, he is heading for his own extinction. That is the check generally imposed on egoism, and thereby the true nature of egoism is made clear. For whereas man, by absorbing the forces of the surrounding world, enables the world to attain a summit in himself, he then has to do consciously what the plant does unconsciously. At the very moment when the plant is in course of imprinting its inner being on its visible form, the power behind the plant leads its egoistic principle over into a new plant. But man, as a self-conscious being and an Ego-bearer, is required to bring about by his own efforts this development in himself. At a certain stage he must be prepared to surrender whatever he has received from outside and to give birth, within his own Ego, to a higher Ego; and this higher Ego will not become hardened, but will enter into a harmonious relationship with the entire world.

The knowledge that a one-sided egoism destroys itself can be verified by ordinary observation of life. One needs only to look at people who are unable to take any active interest in the great and beautiful ordering of nature from which the human organism draws its form and substance. How painful it is for anyone who understands these things to see how some people pass indifferently by the world to which they owe their eyes and ears; how they cut themselves off from the world in which their existence is rooted and wish only to be left alone with their inward brooding. Then we see how this perverted way of living brings its own penalty. Anyone who follows it goes through life in a state of chronic boredom; he pursues one desire after another, not realising that he is seeking satisfaction in vague phantoms, when he should be giving himself out to the world from which his own existence has come about. Anyone who goes through life saying: People are a burden, I have no use for them, they disturb my life, I am too good for this world—anyone who talks like that should merely reflect that he is repudiating the origin of his existence. If he had grown up on a desert island, far from the human society that he regards as not good enough for him, he would have remained dumb and would never have developed the faculties he now has. All that he finds so great and praiseworthy in himself would be absent, were it not for the people he has no use for. He should realise that he has separated himself from his environment by his own wilful choice, and that in fact he owes to his environment the very faculties which now repudiate it.

If a man pursues this course, he not only kills the interest he might have taken in nature and human life, his own life-force declines and he condemns himself to a desolate, dissatisfied existence. All those people who indulge in world-weariness because they find nothing anywhere to interest them, should for once ask themselves: What is my egoism doing to me? Here a cosmic law is indicated. Wherever egoism takes a perverted form, it has a desolating effect on living. That is the good thing about egoism: if it is carried to an extreme, it destroys the egoist.

If now we take the great law that we have gained from studying egoism and apply it to the various faculties of the human soul, we can ask, for example: How does egoism affect the Consciousness Soul, through which man acquires knowledge of the world around him? In other words, when can a piece of knowledge prove fruitful? It will be truly fruitful only if it brings a man into harmony with the rest of the world. This means that the only concepts and ideas that can invigorate the human soul are those drawn from the life of the great outer world, and then only if we are in harmony with the outer world. That is why all ways of knowledge which seek, above all, to reach the great truths of existence, step by step, are so health-giving for the soul, and also, therefore, for the physical body. On the other hand, anything that leads us away from a living connection with the world, as solitary inward brooding does, or anything that brings us into discord with the world, will have a hardening effect.

Here is an appropriate occasion to refer once more to the widely misunderstood saying, "Know thyself!", which has a meaning valid for all epochs. Only when a man realises that he belongs to the whole world, that his Self is not confined within his skin but is spread out over the whole world, over sun and stars, over all earthly creatures, and that this Self has only created an expression of itself within his skin— only if he recognises that he is interwoven with the entire world—only

Human Egoism

then can he make proper use of the saying, "Know thyself!". For self-knowledge is then world-knowledge. A man who fails to realise this is like a finger which imagined it could achieve an individual existence apart from the rest of the organism. Cut it off, and in three weeks it will quite certainly no longer be a finger. The finger has no illusions about that; only man supposes that he could do without any connections with the world. World-knowledge is self-knowledge and self-knowledge is world-knowledge. Any sort of inward brooding is merely a sign that we cannot get away from ourselves. Very great harm is therefore done when in certain theosophical circles today it is said: A solution of the riddle of existence will not be found in the world outside, or in phenomena permeated by the spirit, but in your own self. "Look for God in your own breast"—that is the injunction often heard. "You need not exert yourself to seek for revelations of the cosmic Spirit out there in the universe. You have only to look within yourself; you will find it all there." This kind of instruction does the student very bad service. It makes him proud and egoistic with regard to knowledge. The result is that certain theosophical directives, instead of training a person in selflessness, instead of freeing him from himself and bringing him into relation with the great riddles of existence, have a hardening effect on him. One can appeal to man's pride and vanity by telling him: "You need learn nothing from the world; you will find it all in yourself." We appeal to truth when we show that to be in harmony with the great world can enable a man to become greater in himself and therefore greater in the world.

This applies also to human feeling and to the entire content of the Intellectual Soul, which gains in strength when a man knows how to achieve harmony between himself and the outer world. Strength and power are not acquired by sitting down and brooding all day long over such questions as—What shall I think now? What shall I do? What's that pain I feel coming on again?"—but by opening the heart to everything great and beautiful in our surroundings, and by showing interest and understanding for everything that warms the hearts of others, as well as for their wants and privations. In this way we strengthen the life-forces in the realm of feeling within us; we overcome narrow-minded egoism and we enhance and enrich our Ego by bringing the true form of egoism into harmony with our environment.

This comes out very clearly when we consider the human will and the Consciousness Soul itself. A man who exerts his will only for himself and his own advantage will always feel inwardly dissatisfied. Only when he can see his resolves reflected in the outer world and his will-impulses realised in action—only then can he say that he has brought his willing into harmony with outer events. And here we learn that our inner strength and power are not developed by anything we will for ourselves, but by whatever we will for the outer world and for other people. Our willing becomes reality and its reflection shines back to us. As our eyes are formed by light, so is our strength of soul developed by our actions and activities.

Thus we see how man, as a self-conscious being, is able through a right comprehension of his "I", his Ego, to arrive at harmony between himself and the world around him, until he grows out of himself and accomplishes the birth of what we may call a higher man. In this way he brings forth something in himself, even as a plant on a lower level brings forth out of itself a new being at the moment when it is in danger of becoming hardened in its own existence. That is how we must understand egoism. The human Ego, having been fructified by the surrounding world, brings forth on the heights of existence a new Ego, and will then be ripe to flow out into actions which would otherwise give expression only to worthless demands and useless moral postulates. For only through world-knowledge can the will be fired to act on the world in return. Whatever points may be set out in the programmes of societies, however many societies may have "universal human love" at the head of their programmes, these moral injunctions will have no practical effect.

All the ordinary preaching of human love is as though a stove were standing in a cold room and someone says to it: "Dear stove, your moral duty as a stove is to warm the room". You could go on like that for hours or days—the stove would not be moved to make the room warm. Similarly, men will not be moved by sermons to practise human love, even if you were to preach to them for centuries that men ought to love one another. But bring the human Ego into connection with the content of the whole world, let people participate in the radiance of flowers and in all the beauties of Nature, and you will soon see that this participation is a foundation for the higher participation that can arise between human being and human being.

By gaining knowledge of human beings and human nature, man learns to meet the faults and good qualities of others with understanding. Wisdom of this kind, derived from approaching the world with living insight, passes over into the blood, into action and will. And what we call human love is born from it. Just as babbling to the stove is useless, when what we need to do is simply to bring wood and start a fire, so should we bring to human beings the fuel that will kindle, warm and illuminate their souls; and the fuel required is knowledge of the world, so that understanding of human nature and harmonious consonance

Human Egoism

between the human Ego and the outer world are brought about. Then we shall in fact be kindling human love—a love that can flow from heart to heart and draw human beings together, teaching them that actions performed only for ourselves have a deadly, desolating effect upon us, while actions that have a helpful influence on the lives of others are reflected back to enhance our own strength. Through a right understanding of egoism, accordingly, our Ego is enriched and enabled to develop, if, as far as possible, we realise our own Self in the service of another, and strive to cultivate not only personal feeling, but fellow-feeling, as far as we can. That is how the nature of Egoism is seen by Spiritual Science.

The subject we have touched on today has deeply interested all the thinkers who have pondered seriously on human existence. The nature of egoism was bound to concern outstanding men during the 18th century, a time when man as an individual had broken free from certain ties with his social environment. One of these outstanding men was Goethe. And he has given us a work, *Wilhelm Meister's Years of Apprenticeship* and its sequel *Wilhelm Meister's Years of Travel*, which we can take as an example, as if drawn from the world, of his thoughts on the nature of egoism.

Just as Faust occupied Goethe throughout his life, so did *Wilhelm Meister*. As early as the seventeen-sixties, Goethe felt that he had the task of depicting, in the peculiar life of Wilhelm Meister, a kind of mirror-image of his own life, and it was in his old age, when he was nearing his death, that he completed the *Years of Travel*. It would take us too far to go into the details of *Wilhelm Meister*, but perhaps you will allow me to outline the problem of egoism as we meet it here in Goethe.

A thoroughgoing, refined egoist, one might say, is portrayed here. Wilhelm Meister was born into the merchant class, but he is enough of an egoist to abandon this calling, in spite of the claims of duty. What, then, does he really want? We are shown how he wants to develop his own Self to the highest degree and with the utmost freedom. He has a dim presentiment of becoming some kind of perfected man. Thus Goethe leads Wilhelm Meister through the most varied experiences, so as to show how life works upon this individuality in order to raise it to a higher level. Of course, Goethe is well aware that Wilhelm Meister is driven around by all sorts of circumstances and reaches no definite goal. Hence at one point he calls him a "poor wretch".[49] But at the same time he knows that although a man may have to work his way through folly and errors, he is led by certain forces to a certain goal, or at least along a certain path. It was Goethe's opinion, which never left him, that human life is never completely at the mercy of chance, but is subject, like all things, to laws—indeed, spiritual laws. Therefore Goethe says that the whole human race can be regarded as a great individual, striving upwards and making itself the master of chance.[50]

Goethe's intention, accordingly, is to show Wilhelm Meister as intent always on heightening, enriching and perfecting his Ego. At the same time, he leads Wilhelm Meister into a way of life which is, strictly speaking, at one remove from actuality. The whole character of the 18th century can help us to understand why Wilhelm Meister is led away from pursuing a career in the world of real events and brought into the theatre, where he mingles with people who present an appearance, a picture, of life. Art itself is, in a certain sense, an image of life.

It is not part of immediate reality but raises itself above this reality. Goethe knew very well that the artist, standing alone with his art, is in danger of losing the firm ground of reality from under his feet. It has been well said that the Muse may accompany a man but cannot lead him through life.

To begin with, Wilhelm Meister gives himself over entirely to the forces that belong to art, and especially the art of the theatre, with its beautiful illusions. If we follow the course of his life, we find that he is habitually torn to and fro between dissatisfaction and joy, and these swings of feeling are evident already during his time in the theatre. At last he experiences a kind of model performance of *Hamlet,* and this gives him a certain satisfaction within the limits of the theatrical world. His Ego is enhanced.

Two episodes are particularly important for understanding this first part of the story, the *Years of Apprenticeship,* and they show clearly that Goethe had the nature of egoism at the back of his mind. The first episode concerns little Mignon, who is found by Wilhelm Meister in somewhat dubious company and accompanies him as a wonderful attendant for a while.

Some very significant remarks about Mignon were made to Chancellor von Müller[51] by Goethe in his old age. He referred to Madame von Stael's comment that all the part about Mignon was an episode which did not really belong to the story. Goethe agreed that anyone interested only in the external narrative might say that the Mignon episode could be left out. But it would be quite wrong to suppose, Goethe continued, that the part about Mignon was *only* an episode; in fact, the whole of *Wilhelm Meister* had been written on account of this remarkable figure.

Goethe was apt to express himself somewhat radically in conversation and to say things that are not to be taken literally. But if we go more deeply into the matter, we can come to see why he spoke in this way to

Human Egoism

Chancellor von Müller. In the figure of Mignon—this is not a personal name but means simply "the darling"—we are shown a human being who lives just long enough for the germ of anything that can properly be called egoism to develop in her. The whole psychology of Mignon is most remarkable. In her own naive way she expresses everything that could be called participation in the whole world. She never gives any sign of acting from selfish motives. Things that other people do out of self-interest are done by her quite naturally. She is naive in the sense that egoism has not yet awoken in her. Directly Wilhelm Meister embarks on an episode in his life which breaks his bond of union with Mignon, she fades away and dies, just as a plant withers when it has reached a certain stage in its existence. She is not yet a fully human person, not yet an "Ego"; she represents a childlike naivete in relation to everything in the world around her. She dies as a plant dies, and one could indeed apply to her the lines:

> Not asking why or wherefore blooms the rose,
> Cares not for herself or whether men behold her.

One might say that two apparently identical actions are different when they are performed by different persons! What other people do out of egoism Mignon does naturally, and directly that there could be a question of an egoistic impulse arising in her soul, she dies. That is the enchantment of her character: we have before us a human being without ego-hood who slips through our fingers at the first stirring of egoism within her. And since Goethe was specially interested in egoism in *Wilhelm Meister,* it is quite conceivable that he should have said in effect at the time: What you are looking for in Wilhelm Meister, you will find in his counterpart, Mignon. The impulse that shows itself in the little creature, and dies with her at the moment of its appearance, is the same impulse that plagues Wilhelm Meister with so many difficulties when he tries to develop his Ego, and on account of which he has to go through a complete education in the school of life.

We then find woven into the story of Wilhelm Meister the apparently unconnected part called *Confessions of a Beautiful Soul.* It is known that these confessions are taken almost word for word from a diary kept by Goethe's friend, Susanne von Klettenberg. They show, one might say, the nature of egoism at its highest point. This beautiful soul, Susanne von Klettenberg, rose indeed to high levels, but these confessions bring out the danger of egoism, the reverse side of the enrichment of the Ego, for it is her own development that Susanne von Klettenberg describes.

First, she relates how, like other people, she delighted in the world around her. Then, one day, something awakens in her soul and tells her: "Living within you is something that will bring you nearer to the God within you." These inward experiences have the effect of estranging her from the outer world; she no longer feels any interest in it. But she finds continual joy and blessedness and inward happiness in her experience of communion with what she inwardly calls her "God". She withdraws entirely into her inner life. Yet this beautiful soul cannot escape from the feeling that her chosen way of life is nothing else than a refined form of egoism.

The dawning of this type of spiritual element in the soul, where it estranges a person from the outer world, shuts him off from his environment and makes him cold and heartless towards it, may bring him some satisfaction and a certain happiness, but in the long run it does him no good. By alienating him from the world around him it has a desolating effect on his soul. But this beautiful soul is also an energetic, striving soul, and she goes on from stage to stage.

She is not able to sever herself entirely from the impressions that come from the outer world and can lead to harmony with it. So she is forever seeking the mysteries that underlie the symbols of the various religions, hoping to see reflected there the divinity that had arisen in her soul. But whatever she can experience in these outer forms is not enough for her; she is resolved to go further. Finally, she is led to a remarkable stage in her life. One day she says to herself: Everything human on our earth was not too mean for God to descend and incarnate himself in a man. And at that moment she feels that the outer world is not debased by being only an expression of the spiritual rather than the spiritual itself, or because it represents a decadence of the spiritual; for now she feels that the outer world is permeated by the spirit and that man has no right to detach himself from his environment.

Then another experience comes to her and she says to herself: It was a true event that is said to have taken place in Palestine at the beginning of our era. She enters into this and experiences in herself the whole life of Christ Jesus up to his crucifixion and death. She experiences the divine in herself in such a way that—as she clearly describes—everything which appears to the physical senses as external image recedes and becomes purely spiritual experience; the invisible becomes visible and the inaudible, audible. Now she feels herself united not with an abstract divinity, but with a divine presence belonging to the earthly world. But she has again withdrawn in a certain sense and cannot find her way back into ordinary life. Then something comes to her which enables her to see in every natural object, in every detail and circumstance of daily life, the imprint of the spiritual; and she regards this as a kind of highest stage. And it is characteristic of Goethe that it was for him a kind of confession to be able to communicate the *Confessions of a Beautiful Soul.*

What was it that Goethe wished to indicate here as an important point in Wilhelm Meister's education? Wilhelm Meister was to read the manuscript and be led by it to a higher stage. He was to be shown that a man cannot do enough to develop in himself an active life of soul; he cannot go far and high enough in what may be called intercourse with the spiritual world; but also that to shut himself off from the outer world cannot lead to a satisfying existence, and that he can understand the great world around him only when his own enriched inner being flows out to meet it.

Thus Goethe wishes to show that a man can take the surrounding world just as it is; he will then see it as ordinary and trivial and will remain bound to the commonplace. But then he will perhaps say to himself: All that is commonplace: the spiritual can be found only by looking within oneself. And we can indeed find the spiritual there, on a very high level. But we are then all the more in duty bound, for our own sake, to return to the outer world; and now we find that the commonplace has a spiritual dimension. The same world stands before a trivially minded man and a man who has found the spirit within himself. The former accepts the ordinary trivial world of present-day Monism; the latter, having first enriched his spiritual faculties and developed the appropriate organs in himself, is aware of the spiritual behind everything perceived by the senses. Thus, for Goethe, inner development is an indirect way of gaining knowledge of the world. This is evident, above all, in the soul characterised as Wilhelm Meister. He is helped to progress by the influences that work on him from the hidden side of life.

Towards the end of the *Years of Apprenticeship* we are shown that behind Wilhelm Meister there is something like an occult society, which guides a human being while remaining invisible to him. Some critics have complained that this kind of thing belongs to the 18th century and can have no interest for people today. For Goethe, however, something quite different was involved. He wished to show that Wilhelm Meister's Ego really had to find its way through the various labyrinths of life, and that a certain spiritual guidance of mankind does exist. The "Society of the Tower", by which Wilhelm Meister is guided, was meant to be only the outer garment of spiritual powers and forces by which a man is led, even though the course of his life may lie through "folly and confusion"; and by these invisible powers Wilhelm Meister was guided.

In our time, such things are dismissed with a condescending smile. But in our time, also, the Philistines have acquired the sole right to pass judgment on personalities such as Goethe. Anyone who knows the world will concede that no-one can find more in a man than he has in himself. And anyone could say it in relation to Goethe. But that is just what the Philistine does not say; he believes he has found in Goethe everything there is to find. For he possesses the entire range of wisdom and can survey it from his vantage-point! Naturally, he makes Goethe into a Philistine, but that is not Goethe's fault.

Wilhelm Meister's life is continued in the *Years of Travel.* Both Philistines and non-Philistines have been moved to protest at the lack of composition and the inartistic character of this sequel. Yes, indeed, Goethe served up something rather dreadful here. In his prime, out of his life-experience, he had wanted to show a person finding their way through the labyrinths of life, had wanted to present a mirror-image of himself in a certain sense; and he has told us how this was composed. He had taken great pains over the first part of the *Years of Travel,* but printing began before the later part was finished, and the printer set the type faster than Goethe could write. Goethe then had somehow to sketch out the rest. In earlier years he had written various tales and stories, for example the story of the "Holy Family", the story of the "Nutbrown Maiden", the "Tale of the New Melusine", and others. All these are included in the *Years of Travel* volume, although never intended for it. Goethe inserted these stories at various points and made quick transitions between them. Obviously, anything like orderly composition was ruled out; but still the work did not go fast enough.

Goethe had various other writings left over from earlier years, and these he now gave to his secretary, Eckermann, saying: "Slip in somewhere whatever can be slipped in!". So Eckermann patched in these remnants, and naturally the separate items are often very loosely connected. Hence it can well be said that this is an entirely formless work, and anyone is at liberty to judge it in this way from an artistic standpoint. But, after all, not a line of it was written by Eckermann. It is all by Goethe, and throughout he was giving expression to experiences of his own, with the figure of Wilhelm Meister constantly before him. Thus he was able to bring in events from his own life which had set their mark on his soul. And since Wilhelm Meister is a reflected image of himself, the various episodes meander through the story even as they had meandered through his own life, and the picture we gain from them is by no means irrelevant.

It has been said that the narrative lacks tension and is repeatedly

Human Egoism

interrupted by sagely discourses. Some people criticise the book from the ground up without having read it. They are, of course, right from their own point of view, but it is not the only one. We can learn an immense amount from these *Years of Travel* if we can muster the interest and the goodwill to raise ourselves to the level of the experiences from which Goethe learnt so much. And that is something. Must every piece of writing be skilfully composed if it can be of service to us in some other way? Is a lack of formal design so fatal? Perhaps the wealth of wisdom in *Wilhelm Meister* is fatal for those who know everything and have nothing more to learn.

It is precisely in this second part of *Wilhelm Meister* that we find described in a wonderful way how the Ego can rise to ever higher levels and become the peak of existence. We are shown in a particularly beautiful way how Wilhelm Meister takes his son Felix to a remarkable educational establishment. This, too, has been condemned by the Philistines. They have not stopped to think that Goethe had no intention of presenting this establishment as though it existed somewhere or other in the real world. He wished to give a kind of symbolic survey of the nature of education in his "pedagogical province".

People who visit this establishment are surprised to see how the life of the soul is given expression in certain gestures. In one gesture the hands are folded on the breast and the eyes turned upwards. In another, the hands are clasped behind the back while the pupils stand side by side. Especially significant is the gesture which gives an impression of the soul bowing towards the earth. If questions are asked about the meaning of all this, one is told that the boys are taught to kindle in their souls the "three venerations", whereby the soul's development can be carried to ever higher levels. The three venerations are presented as the most important of all educational principles. First, a man must learn to look up with veneration to what is above him. Then he must learn to venerate what lies beneath him, so that he may realise how he himself has grown up from it. Then he must learn to venerate what stands beside him as equality between man and man, for only thus can he learn to venerate his own Ego in the right way. By these means he will be brought into harmony with the world around him and egoism cannot go astray.

We are then shown how the most important religions are to carry their influences into the human soul. The folk or ethnic religions should take the form of gods or spirits standing above man. The philosophical religions, as they could be called, are to inculcate veneration for our equals. And the teaching that leads us down into existence and enables us to look with proper veneration on death, sorrow and the hindrances in the world—this teaching, though it can easily be despised, leads to a right understanding of the Christian religion. For it is emphasised that the Christian religion shows how God came down into a physical body, took on himself all the misery of life and went through everything human. Veneration for what is below us should especially promote a right understanding of the Christian religion.

Thus the development of the human being is set before us with precision. Goethe describes how Wilhelm Meister is led to a kind of temple, where deeply significant pictures of the three religions are brought before the souls of the pupils from their earliest youth, and we are shown how everything in this utopian school is intended to produce a harmonious whole. But the school gives expression even more to the wise principle that from his earliest years a human being should grow up in such a way that, on the one hand, he finds harmony with his environment, while, on the other, he finds it possible to lead his Ego to ever-greater heights.

This principle is applied to all details. For example, a boy's age is not indicated by the clothes he wears. He is offered a varied range of garments and has to choose those he prefers. In this way the individual characteristics of the pupils are brought out. Moreover, since a kind of *esprit de corps* is always apt to develop, with the result that a weaker boy will imitate a stronger by choosing the same outfit, to the detriment of his own individuality, the rule is that garments are exchanged for others at frequent intervals. In brief, Goethe wished to show how the growing boy should be educated, even down to his gestures and clothes, in a way that will lead him to a life in harmony with the world around him, while promoting his inner freedom as an individual.

It has been said that all this is a fantasy and that nothing like it has ever existed. But Goethe meant to imply only that the plan could be realised somewhere at some time; the thoughts in question would flow out into the "all and everywhere" and would find an embodiment when and where they could. Those who think this impossible might be advised to read Fichte;[52] he set a high ideal before his students, but he knew what he was doing, and to those who called themselves realists, while knowing little about reality, he said: We know as well as you do, and perhaps better, that ideals cannot be realised immediately in ordinary life, but ideals must be there, in order to act as regulators in life and to be transmuted into living. That must be emphasised ever and again. And of those who reject all ideals, Fichte said that in the reckoning of Providence they were left out; but may a good God—he added—grant them rain and sunshine at the right times, a good digestion and, where possible, good thoughts! This saying could be turned against those

Human Egoism

who assert that the educational establishment in Goethe's *Wilhelm Meister* could never exist in reality. It could exist, both in its principles and in its details, if there were people ready to give effect to such principles in a setting of everyday life.

A second episode in the *Years of Travel* introduces a remarkable personality, Makarie, who exemplifies in the highest degree a union of the individual Ego with the great Self of the world. Goethe shows us here a personality who is inwardly awakened and has developed the spirit in herself to such an extent that she lives in the spirit that permeates the world. The liberation of her inner powers gives her the knowledge that an expert astronomer acquires from calculating the courses of the stars. The highest spiritual-scientific researches are indicated by Goethe when he describes how through spiritual science the soul can enter into the life of the universe, and how self-knowledge can become world-knowledge and world-knowledge, self-knowledge. Thus in a series of pictures we are shown how the human self must pursue its development. Rightly understood, *Wilhelm Meister* is from beginning to end an example of how the development of man is related to the nature of egoism.

If we find in a writer an exposition of a problem so important for Spiritual Science, this is for us a further proof—already apparent in our considerations of *Faust,* the *Tale of the Green Snake and the Beautiful Lily,* and *Pandora*[53] —that in Goethe we have a genius who is at one with our Spiritual Science in its true sense. Goethe himself speaks in this sense when he says, in effect: We can grasp the nature of egoism only if we know that the wisdom of the cosmos had to lead man out of spiritual existence to the point where he could fall into the temptations of egoism. If this possibility had not been open to him, he could not have become the flower of all that surrounds him in the outer world. But if he succumbs to the temptations of egoism, he incurs a sentence of death on himself. The wisdom of the cosmos has ensured that everything good in the world can be overturned and appear in man as freedom, but directly he misuses his freedom and overturns himself, a measure of self-correction comes in.

Here again we have a chapter which shows us how everything bad and sinful in human nature, if we consider it from a higher standpoint, can be transmuted into good—into a pledge of man's eternal, ever-ascending progress. And so, if we are not afraid to descend into the depths of pain and evil, all the teachings of spiritual science will lead us eventually to the heights, and will confirm the beautiful words which resound to us from the wisdom and poetry of ancient Greece:

Metamorphoses of the Soul

Man is the shadow of a dream, but when
The sun-ray, Heaven-sent,
Shines in upon him, then
His day is bright,
And all his life transfused with sheer delight.[54]

LECTURE 8
Buddha and Christ[55]

Berlin, 2nd December, 1909

Ever since its foundation, the spiritual-scientific movement has suffered from being confused with all sorts of other tendencies and strivings of the present day. Particularly it is accused of trying to transplant certain eastern spiritual currents, especially that of Buddhism, into the culture of the West. Hence our subject today has a special relevance for spiritual research: we are going to consider the significance of the Buddhist religion on the one hand and that of Christianity on the other, from the standpoint of Spiritual Science. Those who have often attended my lectures here will know that we intend a study in the scientific sense, ranging widely over world-events from the point of view of spiritual life.

Anyone who has thought at all seriously about Buddhism will know that its founder, Gautama Buddha, always refused to answer questions concerning the evolution of the world and the foundations of our human existence. He wished to speak only about the means whereby a man could come to a way of existence that would be satisfying in itself. This fact alone should be enough to distinguish Buddhism from Spiritual Science, for Spiritual Science never refuses to speak about world origins and the great facts of evolution. And if one particular aspect of Spiritual Science is being more and more confused with Buddhism— namely our treatment of repeated earth-lives and the working of spiritual causes from earlier lives into later ones—it is strange that Spiritual Science should be charged on this account with being a form of Buddhism. By now people should surely have grasped that Spiritual Science is not concerned with names but with ascertainable truth, independently of any name that may be given to it. The fact that the doctrine of reincarnation or repeated earth-lives is to be found among the ideas of Gautama Buddha, though in a quite different form, has no more significance for Theosophy or Spiritual Science than the

119

Metamorphoses of the Soul

fact that the elements of geometry are found in Euclid. Just as it would be absurd to accuse a geometry teacher of practising "Euclidism", so is it absurd to bring a charge of Buddhism against Spiritual Science because it has a doctrine of reincarnation and similar ideas are to be found in the Buddha. At the same time we must make it clear that Spiritual Science provides a means of testing the spiritual sources of every religion—including Christianity, the basis of European culture, on the one hand, and Buddhism on the other.

The notion that Spiritual Science wants to be "Buddhism" is not confined to persons who know nothing of Theosophy. Even the great orientalist, Max Muller,[56] who has done so much to make oriental religions better known in Europe, cannot rid himself of it. In discussing it with another writer he used the following analogy. If, he says, a man were to be seen somewhere with a pig that was a good grunter, no-one would be surprised; but if a man could mimic the grunting to perfection, people would gather round and look on it as a miracle! By the grunting pig Max Muller means the real Buddhism, which by then had become known in Europe. But its teaching, he continues, was attracting no attention, while false Buddhism, or what he calls "Madame Blavatsky's theosophical swindle",[57] was gaining wide acceptance.

The analogy is not very happy. Even apart from the fact that it is hardly polite to represent the true Buddhist teaching, which came to birth with so much travail, by the grunting of a pig, the analogy implies that Madame Blavatsky succeeded extremely well in producing an exact imitation of Buddhism. Madame Blavatsky deserves credit for having set the ball rolling, but nowadays very few thoughtful theosophists believe that she was successful in reproducing true, genuine Buddhism. Just as a teacher of geometry is not required to produce a replica of Euclid, so a teacher of Theosophy is not required to reproduce Buddhism.

If we wish to immerse ourselves in the spirit of Buddhism in the sense of Spiritual Science, so that we may then compare it with the spirit of Christianity, we had better not proceed immediately to its deeper doctrines, which can readily be interpreted in various ways. We will rather try to gain an impression of its significance from its whole way of thinking and forming ideas. Our best course is to start with a document that is very highly regarded in Buddhist circles: the questions put by King Milinda to the Buddhist sage, Nagasena.[58] Here we find a conversation which brings out the inner character of the Buddhist way of thinking. Milinda, the mighty and brilliant King who has never been defeated by a sage, being always able to repulse any objections brought against his own ideas, wants to converse with Nagasena about

Buddha and Christ

the significance of the immortal, eternal element in human nature which passes from one incarnation to the next.

Nagasena asks the King: "How did you come here—on foot or in a chariot?" "In a chariot", the King replies. "Now", says Nagasena, "let us inquire into this question of the chariot—what is it? Is the axle the chariot? No. Is it the wheel? No. Is it the yoke? No. And so", says Nagasena, "we may go through all the parts of the chariot; none of them is the chariot. Yet the chariot we have before us is made up entirely of these separate parts. 'Chariot' is only a name for the sum total of these parts. If we set aside the parts, we have nothing left but the name."

Nagasena's aim in all this is to lead the eye away from the physical world. He wants to show that the composite form designated by a "name" does not actually exist as such in the physical world, so that he may thus bring out the worthlessness and meaninglessness of the physical sense-perceptible as the sum of its parts.

In order to make the point of this parable quite clear, Nagasena says: "Thus it is also with the composite form that is man, which passes from one earth-life to another. Is it the hands and head and legs that pass from one earth-life to another? No. Is it what you are doing today or will do tomorrow? No. What then is it that constitutes a human being? The name and the form. But just as with the chariot, when we look on the sum of the parts we only have a name. We have nothing more than the parts!"

We can bring out the argument even more clearly by turning to another parable that Nagasena sets before King Milinda. The King speaks: "You say, O wise Nagasena, that what passes from one incarnation to another are the name and form of the human being. When they appear again on earth in a new incarnation, are they the name and form of the same being?" Nagasena answers: "Behold, your mango tree is bearing fruit. Then a thief comes and steals the fruit. The owner of the mango-tree cries: 'You have stolen my fruit!' 'It is not your fruit', the thief replies. 'Your fruit was the one you buried in the ground, where it dissolved. The fruit now growing on the tree has the same name, but it is not your fruit.' " Nagasena then continued: "Yes, it is true—the fruit has the same name and form, but it is not the same fruit. Yet the thief can still be punished for his theft. So it is with what re-appears in an earthly life compared with what appeared in previous lives. It is only because the owner of the mango-tree planted a fruit in the earth that fruit now grows on the tree. Hence we must regard the fruit as his property. It is similar with the deeds and destiny of a man's new life on earth: we must look on them as the effects, the fruit, of his previous life. But what appears is something new, as is the fruit on the mango-tree."

In this way Nagasena sought to dissolve everything that makes up an earth-life, in order to show how only its effects pass over into the next life on earth.

This approach can give us a much better idea of the whole spirit of Buddhist teaching than we could gain from its general principles, for these—as I said—can be interpreted in various ways. If we allow the spirit of Nagasena's parables to work upon us, we can see clearly enough how the Buddist teacher wishes to draw his disciples away from everything that stands here before us as a separate human Ego, a definite personality; how he wishes to direct attention above all to the idea that, although what appears in a new incarnation is indeed an effect of the previous personality, we have no right to speak in any true sense of a coherent Ego which passes on from one earth-life to the next.

If now we turn from Buddhism to Christianity, we could—though it has never been done—rewrite Nagasena's examples in a Christian sense, somewhat as follows. Let us suppose that King Milinda has arisen from death as a Christian and that the ensuing conversation is permeated, with the spirit of Christianity. Nagasena would then have to say: "Look at your hand! Is the hand a man? No—the hand alone does not make a man. But if you cut off the hand from the man, it will decay, and in two or three weeks it will no longer be a hand. What then is it makes the hand a hand? It is the man who makes the hand a hand! Is the heart a man? No! Is the heart something self-sufficient? No, for if we separate the heart from the man, it will soon cease to be heart—and the man will soon cease to be a man. Hence it is the man who makes the heart a heart and the heart that makes the man a man. The man is a man living on earth only because he has the heart as an instrument. Thus in the living human organism we have parts which in themselves are nothing; they exist only in relation to our entire make-up. And if we reflect on how it is that the separate parts cannot exist on their own, we find that we must look beyond them to some invisible agency which rules over them, holds them together and uses them as instruments to serve its needs."

Nagasena could then return to his parable of the chariot and might say, speaking now in a Christian sense: "True, the axle is not the chariot, for with the axle alone you cannot drive. True, the wheels are not the chariot, for with the wheels alone you cannot drive. True, the yoke is not the chariot, for with the yoke alone you cannot drive. True, the seat is not the chariot, for with the seat alone you cannot drive. And although the chariot is only a name for the assembly of parts, you do

Buddha and Christ

not drive with the parts but with something that is not the parts. So the 'name' does stand for something specific! It leads us to something that is not in any of the parts."

Thus the spirit of Buddhist teaching aims at diverting attention from the visible in order to get beyond it, and it denies the significance of anything visible. The Christian approach sees the parts of a chariot, or of any other object, in such a way that the mind is directed towards the whole. From this contrast we can see that both the Christian and the Buddhist approach to the outer world have definite consequences. And if now we follow the Buddhist approach to its logical conclusion, its consequences will be plain to see.

A man, a Buddhist, stands before us. He plays his part in the world and performs various actions. His Buddhist teaching tells him that everything around him is worthless. The nothingness and non-existence of everything visible is impressed upon him. Then he is told that he ought to free himself from dependence on this nothingness in order to reach a real, higher state of being. With this aim in mind he should avert his gaze from the sense-world and from everything he could learn about it through his human faculties. Turn away from the sense-world! For if we reduce to name and form everything offered by the sense-world, its nothingness is revealed. No truth is to be found in the sense-world displayed before us!

What does the Christian way of thinking make of all this? It regards any single part of the human organism not as a separate unit, but as embraced by a real, unified whole. The hand, for example, is a hand only because man uses it as a hand. Here the thing we see points directly to something behind it. This way of thinking thus leads to findings very different from those that derive from the Buddhist way. Hence we can say: A man stands before us. He exists as a man only because behind him stands a spiritual man who activates his constituent parts and is the directing source of whatever he does or accomplishes. That which animates the parts of his organism and lives in them has poured itself into the visible being, where it experiences the fruits of action. From thus experiencing the sense-world it extracts something we may call a "result", and this is carried over into the next incarnation, the next life on earth. Behind the external man there is this active man, this doer, who does not reject the outer world but handles it in such a way that its fruits are garnered and carried over to the next life.

If we look at this question of repeated earth-lives from the standpoint of Spiritual Science, we must say: For Buddhism, the principle that holds a man together during life does not endure; only his actions work on into his next earth-life. For Christianity, the principle that holds

Metamorphoses of the Soul

a man together is a complete Ego; and this Ego endures. It carries over into the next earth-life all the fruits of the preceding one.

Hence we see that what keeps these two world-outlooks decisively apart is the quite definite difference between their respective ways of thinking, and this counts for much more than theories or principles. If in our time people were not so wedded to theories about everything, they would find it easier to recognise the character of a spiritual movement from its typical concepts.

All this is connected with a final difference between the Christian and Buddhist outlooks. The core of Buddhist doctrine has been set forth in immensely significant words by the founder of Buddhism himself. Now this lecture is truly not being given in order to promote opposition to the great originator of Buddhist teaching. My intention is to describe the Buddhist world-outlook quite objectively. It is precisely Spiritual Science that is the right instrument for penetrating without sympathy or antipathy into the heart of the various spiritual movements in the world.

The Buddha-legend brings out clearly enough, even if in a pictorial form, what the founder of Buddhism was aiming at. We are told that Gautama Buddha, the son of King Suddhodana, was brought up in a royal palace, where everything around him was designed to enhance the quality of life. Throughout his youth he knew nothing of human suffering or sorrow; he was surrounded by nothing but happiness, pleasure and diversions. One day he left the palace, and for the first time the pains and sorrows, all the shadow-side of human life, met him face to face. He saw an old man withering away; he saw a man stricken with disease; above all, he saw a corpse. Hence it came to him that life must be very different from what he had seen of it in the royal palace. He saw now that human life is bound up with pain and suffering.

It weighed heavily on the Buddha's great soul that human life entails suffering and death, as he had seen them in the sick man, the aged man and the corpse. For he said to himself: "What is life worth if old age, sickness and death are inescapably part of it?"

These reflections gave rise to the Buddha's monumental doctrine of suffering, which he summarised in the words: Birth is suffering, old age is suffering, illness is suffering, death is suffering. All existence is filled with suffering. That we cannot always be united with that which we love—this is how Buddha himself later developed his teaching—is suffering. That we have to be united with that which we do not love, is suffering. That we cannot attain in every sphere of life what we want and desire, is suffering. Thus there is suffering wherever we look. Even though the word "suffering", as used by the Buddha, does not have

Buddha and Christ

quite the meaning it has for us today, it did mean that everywhere man is exposed to things that come against him from outside and against which he can muster no effective strength. Life is suffering, and therefore, said the Buddha, we must ask what the cause of suffering is. Then there came before his soul the phenomenon he called "thirst for existence". If there is suffering everywhere in the world then man is bound to encounter suffering as soon as he enters this world of suffering. Why does he have to suffer in this way? The reason is that he has an urge, a thirst, for incarnation in this world. The passionate desire to pass from the spiritual world into a physical-corporeal existence and to perceive the physical world—therein lies the basic cause of human existence. Hence there is only one way to gain release from suffering: to fight against the thirst for existence. And this can be done if we learn to follow the eight-fold path, in accordance with the teaching of the great Buddha. This is usually taken to embrace correct views, correct aims, correct speech, correct actions, correct living, correct endeavour, correct thoughts, and correct meditation. This taking hold of life in the correct way and relating oneself correctly to life, will gradually enable a man to kill off the desire for existence, and will finally lead him so far that he no longer needs to descend into a physical incarnation and so is released from existence and the suffering that pervades it. Thus the four noble truths, as the Buddha called them, are:

1. Knowledge of suffering
2. Knowledge of the causes of suffering
3. Knowledge of the need to end suffering
4. Knowledge of the means to end suffering

These are the four holy truths that were proclaimed by the Buddha in his great sermon at Benares in the fifth or sixth century, B.C., after his illumination under the Bodhi tree.

Release from the sufferings of existence—that is what Buddhism puts in the foreground, above all else. And that is why it can be called a religion of redemption, in the most eminent sense of the word, a religion of release from the sufferings of existence, and therefore— since all existence is bound up with suffering—of release from the cycle of repeated lives on earth.

This is quite in keeping with the conceptions described in the first part of this lecture. For if a thought directed to the outer world finds only nothingness, if that which holds together the parts of anything is only name and form, and if nothing carries over the effects of one incarnation into the next, then we can say that "true existence" can

Metamorphoses of the Soul

be achieved only if a man passes beyond everything he encounters in the outer sense-world.

It would obviously not be right to call Christianity a "religion of redemption" in the same sense as Buddhism. If we wish to put Christianity in its right relationship to Buddhism from this standpoint, we could call it a "religion of rebirth". For Christianity starts from a recognition that everything in an individual life bears fruits which are of importance and value for the innermost being of man and are carried over into a new life, where they are lived out on a higher level of fulfilment. All that we extract from a single life becomes more and more nearly perfect, until at last it appears in a spiritual form. Even the least significant elements in our existence, if they are taken up by the spiritual and given new life on an ever more perfect level, can be woven into the spiritual. Nothing in human existence is null and void, for it goes through a resurrection when the spirit has transformed it in the right way.

It is as a religion of rebirth, of the resurrection of the best that we have experienced, that we should look on Christianity—a religion for which nothing we encounter is worthless, but is rather a building-stone for the great edifice that is to arise by a bringing together of everything spiritual in the sense-world around us. Buddhism is a religion of release from existence, while Christianity is a religion of rebirth on a spiritual level. This is evident in their ways of thinking about things great and small and in their final principles.

If we look for the causes of this contrast, we shall find them in the quite opposite characteristics of Western and Eastern culture. The fundamental difference between them can be put quite simply. All genuine Eastern culture which has not yet been fertilised by the West is non-historical, whereas all Western culture is historical. And that is ultimately the difference between the Christian and the Buddhist outlooks. The Christian outlook is historical: it recognises not only that repeated earth-lives occur but that they form an historical sequence, so that what is first experienced on an imperfect level can rise in the course of further incarnations to ever higher and more nearly perfect levels. While Buddhism sees release from earth-existence in terms of rising to Nirvana, Christianity sees its aim as a continuing process of development, whereby all the products and achievements of single lives shine forth in ever-higher stages of perfection, until, permeated by the spirit, they experience resurrection at the end of earth-existence.

Buddhism is non-historical, quite in the sense of the cultural background out of which it grew. It turns its gaze to earlier and later incarnations of man and sees him in opposition to the external world. It

Buddha and Christ

never asks whether in earlier times man may have stood in a different relationship to the external world or whether in the future this relationship may again be different—though these are questions that Christianity does ask. So Buddhism comes to the view that man's relationship to the world in which he incarnates is always the same. Driven into incarnation by his thirst for existence, he enters a world of suffering; it matters not whether the world called forth this same thirst in him in the past or will do so in the future. Suffering, and again suffering, is what he is bound always to experience during life on earth. So earth-lives are repeated, and Buddhism never truely connects them with any idea of historical development. That is why Buddhism can see its Nirvana, its state of bliss, as attainable only by withdrawing from the ever-repeated cycle of lives on earth, and why it has to regard the world itself as the source of human suffering. For it says that if we ever enter the physical world, we are bound to suffer: the sense-world cannot but bring us suffering.

That is not Christian, for the Christian outlook is historical through and through. It recognises that man, in being born again and again, faces an external world; but if these encounters bring him suffering, or leave him unsatisfied, deprived of an inwardly harmonious existence, this is not because earthly life is always such that man must suffer, but because he has related himself wrongly to the external world.

Christianity and the Old Testament both point to a definite event, as a result of which man has developed his inner life in such a way that he can make his existence in the world around him a source of suffering. Suffering is not inflicted on us by the world we perceive through our eyes and ears, the world in which we are incarnated; humanity once developed something within itself which placed it in a wrong relation to the world. And as this is inherited from generation to generation, it is still the cause of human suffering today. In the Christian sense we can say that from the beginning of the earth-existence human beings have not had a right relation to the outer world.

This comparison can be extended to the fundamental doctrines of the two religions. Buddhism emphasises again and again that the outer world is Maya, illusion. Christianity, on the contrary, says: Man may indeed believe that what he sees of the outer world is an illusion, but that is because his organs are so constituted that he cannot see through the external veil to the spiritual world. The outer world is not an illusion; the illusion has its source in the limitations of human seeing. Buddhism says: Look at the rocks around you; look where the lightning flashes and the thunder rolls—it is all Maya, the great illusion. Christian thinking would reply that it is wrong to call the outer world an illusion. No, it

Metamorphoses of the Soul

is man who has not yet found the way to open the spiritual senses—his spirit-eyes and spirit-ears, in Goethe's words—which could show him how the outer world is to be seen in its true form. Christianity, accordingly, looks for a pre-historical event which has prevented the human heart from forming a true picture of the outer world. And human development through a series of incarnations must be seen as a means whereby man can regain, in a Christian sense, his spirit-eyes and spirit-ears in order to see the external world as it really is. Repeated earth-lives are therefore not meaningless: they are the path which will enable man to look at the outer world—from which Buddhism wishes to liberate him—and to see it irradiated by the spirit. To overcome the physical appearance of the world by acquiring the spiritual vision that man does not yet possess, and to dispel the human error whereby the outer world can seem to be only Maya—that is the innermost impulse of Christianity.

In Christianity, therefore, we do not find a great teacher who, as in Buddhism, tells us that the world is a source of suffering and that we must get away from it into another world, the quite different world of Nirvana. Christianity presents a powerful impulse to lead the world forward: the Christ, who has given us the strongest indication of the forces that man can develop out of his inner life—forces that will enable him to make use of every incarnation in such a way that its fruits will be carried into every succeeding incarnation through his own powers. The incarnations are not to cease in order to open the way to Nirvana; but all that we can acquire in them is to be used and developed in order that it may experience resurrection in the spiritual sense.

Herein lies the deepest distinction between the non-historical philosophy of Buddhism and the historical outlook of Christianity. Christianity looks back to a *Fall* of man as the source of pain and suffering and onward to a *Resurrection* for their healing. We cannot gain freedom from pain and suffering by renouncing existence, but only by making good the error which has placed man in a false relationship with the surrounding world. If we correct this error, we shall indeed see that the sense-perceptible world dissolves like a cloud before the sun, and also that all our actions and experiences within it can be resurrected on the spiritual plane.

Christianity is thus a doctrine of reincarnation, of resurrection, and only in that light may we place it beside Buddhism. This, however, involves contrasting the two faiths in the sense of Spiritual Science and entering into the deepest impulses of both.

All that I have said in general terms can be substantiated down to the smallest details. For example, we can find in Buddhism something

Buddha and Christ

like the Sermon on the Mount in the Matthew Gospel:

He that hears the law—that is, the law imparted by the Buddha—is blessed. He who raises himself above the passions is blessed. He who can live in loneliness is blessed. He who can live with the creatures of the world and do them no harm is blessed. And so on.

Thus we could regard the Buddhist beatitudes as a counterpart of the beatitudes in the Sermon on the Mount. We have only to understand them in the right way. Let us compare them with the text of the beatitudes of the Sermon on the Mount in St. Matthew's Gospel.[59] There we hear at the beginning the powerful words: "Blessed are they who are beggars for the spirit, for they will find within themselves the kingdom of heaven." It is not said only "Blessed are they who hear the law"; there is an addition. We are told: Blessed are the poor in spirit, so that they have to beg for it, for "theirs is the kingdom of heaven." What does that mean? We can understand such a saying only if we keep before our souls the whole historical character of the Christian outlook.

First of all, we must remember that all the faculties of the human soul have a history; they have evolved. Spiritual Science takes this word "evolved" very seriously, as meaning that what is there today has not been there always. It tells us that what we call our intellect, our scientific way of thinking, did not exist in primitive times; in place of it there was something we might call a dim, hazy clairvoyance. The way in which we now achieve knowledge of the world was unknown to these early people. But there dwelt in them a kind of primitive wisdom which went far beyond anything we have been able to establish today. Anyone who understands history knows that such a primitive wisdom did exist. In those early times human beings did not know how to build machines or railway engines, or how to dominate their environment with the aid of natural forces, but their vision of the divine-spiritual foundations of the world went far beyond our present knowledge.

This vision did not come from thinking things out. Men could not then proceed as modern science does. They were given inspirations, revelations, which arose dimly in their souls. They were not wholly conscious of them, but they could recognise them as true reflections of the spiritual world and of the ancient wisdom. But as in the course of evolution man passed from life to life, he was destined to lose the old hazy clairvoyance and the ancient wisdom and to learn to grasp things with his intellect. In the future he will unite the two faculties: he will be able to look clairvoyantly into the spiritual world while retaining the forms of modern knowledge. Today we are living in a transition stage. The old clairvoyance has been lost, and what we now are has

Metamorphoses of the Soul

developed in the course of time. How has man reached the point of being able, as a self-conscious being, to get to know the world through his intellect? In particular, when did self-consciousness first come to man?

It was at the time—though world-evolution is not usually interpreted so exactly—when Christ Jesus appeared on earth. Men were at a turning-point given for what has produced the finest achievements of our own time. The coming of the Christ into human evolution marked the transition from the old to the new. When John the Baptist proclaimed, "The Kingdom of Heaven is at hand",[60] he was simply using a technical expression for the experience that would come to men when they began to gain knowledge of the world through their own self-consciousness and no longer through inspirations. The Baptist's call means that knowledge of the world in terms of concepts and ideas is near at hand. Men are no longer dependent on the old clairvoyance, but can now investigate the world for themselves. And the most powerful impulse for this new way of knowledge was given by Christ Jesus.

Hence there is a deep meaning in the very first words of the Sermon on the Mount. They might be interpreted: Men are now at the stage where they are beggars for the spirit. In the past they had clairvoyant vision and could look into the spiritual world. That time is over. But a time will come when man, through the inner force of his Ego, will be able to find a substitute for the old clairvoyance through the Word which will reveal itself within him. Blessed, accordingly, are not only those who in ancient times gained the spirit through twilight inspirations, but also those who no longer have clairvoyance because evolution has brought them to that stage. They are indeed not unblest, those who are beggars for the spirit because they have lost the spirit. Blessed are they, for theirs is that which reveals itself through the Ego and can be achieved through their own self-consciousness.

Further we read: "Blessed are they who suffer", for although the outer sense-world is a cause of suffering because of our relationship to it, the time has now come when man, if he will grasp his self-consciousness and unfold the forces which dwell in his Ego, will come to know the remedy for his suffering. Within himself he will find the possibility of consolation, for the time has come when any external consolation loses significance, because the Ego is to have the strength to find within itself the remedy for suffering. Blessed are they who can no longer find in the outer world all that was once found there. That is also the highest meaning of the beatitude, "Blessed are they who thirst after justice, for they shall be filled." Within the Ego itself will be found a source of justice that will compensate for the injustice in the world.

Buddha and Christ

So it is that Christ Jesus points the way to the human Ego, to the divine element in man. Take into your inner being that which lives in the Christ as a prefiguration; then you will find the strength to carry over from one incarnation to another the fruits of your lives on earth. It is important for life in the spiritual world that you should master what can be experienced in earthly existence.

Bearing on this is an event which in the first instance is one of suffering for Christianity—the death of Christ Jesus, the Mystery of Golgotha. This death is of greater significance than ordinary death; Christ here establishes death as the starting-point of an immortal, invincible life. This death is not merely as though Christ wished to free himself from life; he suffers it because from it works an ascending power, and because out of this death there is to flow eternal life.

This was felt by those who lived in the early centuries of Christianity, and it will be recognised more and more widely when the Christ Impulse is better understood. Then people will understand how it was that six centuries before Christ one of the greatest of men left his palace, saw a dead body and formed the judgment—death is suffering, release from death is salvation—and resolved that he would have no more to do with anything that lay under the dominion of death. Six centuries go by until the Christ comes, and after six more centuries have passed a symbol is raised which will be understood only in the future. What is this symbol?

It was not a Buddha, not a chosen person, but simple folk who went and saw the symbol; saw the cross raised and a dead body upon it. For them, death was not suffering, nor did they turn away from it; they saw in the body a pledge of eternal life, a sign of that which conquers death and points away from everything in the sense-world.

The noble Buddha saw a corpse; he turned away from the sense-world and decided that death is suffering. The simple folk who looked upon the cross and the body did not turn away from the sight: for them it was testimony that from this earthly death there springs eternal life. So it was that six hundred years before the founding of Christianity the Buddha stood before the corpse, and six hundred years after the coming of Christ simple folk saw the symbol which expressed for them what had come about through the founding of Christianity. At no other time has there been such a turning-point in the evolution of mankind. If we look at these things objectively, we come to see even more clearly wherein lie the greatness and significance of Buddhism.

As we have said, man was originally endowed with a primal wisdom, and in the course of successive incarnations this wisdom was gradually lost. The appearance of the great Buddha marks the end of an old epoch of evolution; it provides the strongest historical evidence that men had lost the old wisdom, the old knowledge, and this explains the turning away from life. The Christ is the starting-point of a new evolution, which sees the sources of life eternal in this earthly life.

In our time this important fact concerning human evolution is still not clearly understood. That is why it can happen today that men of fine and noble nature, unable to gain from modern viewpoints what they need for their inner life, turn to something different and find release in Buddhism. And Buddhism does show in a certain sense how a man can be lifted up out of sense-existence and through a certain unfolding of his inner forces can rise above himself. But this can occur only because the greatest impulse and innermost source of Christianity is still so little understood.

Spiritual Science should be the instrument for penetrating ever more deeply into the concepts and outlook of Christianity. And precisely the idea of evolution, to which Spiritual Science does full justice, will be able to lead men to an intimate grasp of Christianity. Spiritual Science can therefore cherish the hope that a rightly understood Christianity will stand out ever more clearly from all misinterpretations of it, without transplanting Buddhism into our time. Any attempt to do this would indeed be shortsighted, for anyone who understands the circumstances of spiritual life in Europe will know that even those movements which are apparently opposed to Christianity have drawn their whole armoury of weapons from Christianity itself. There could have been no Darwin or Haeckel[61] —grotesque as this sounds—if a Christian education had not made it possible for them to think as they thought; if the forms of thought had not been ready for those who, after a Christian education, use them to attack, so to speak, their own mother. What these people say, and the tone of voice in which they say it, are often apparently directed against Christianity, but it is Christian education that enables them to think in this way. It would be unpromising, to say the least, for anyone to try to graft something Oriental into our culture, for it would contradict all the conditions of spiritual life in the West. All we need to do is to get a clear grasp of the fundamental teachings of the two religions.

A more exact study of contemporary spiritual life will indeed bring out such a lack of clarity within it, that men of the highest philosophical eminence are impelled to reject life and are thus moved to sympathy with the thoughts of Buddhism. We have an example of this in Schopenhauer:[62] the whole temper of his life had something Buddhistic about it. For example, he says that the highest type of man is he whom we may call a "saint"; a man who in his life has overcome everything that the outer world can offer. He merely exists in his body, deriving no

Buddha and Christ

ideals from the world around him; he has no aim or purpose, but simply waits for the time when his body will be destroyed, so that every trace of his connection with the sense-world will have vanished. By turning away from the sense-world he nullifies his own sense-life, so that nothing may remain of all that leads in life from fear to suffering, from suffering to terror, from passion to pain.

This is a projection of Buddhist feeling into the West, and we must recognise that it comes about because the deepest impulse in Christianity is not clearly understood. What have we gained through Christianity? From the purest form of the Christian impulse we have gained precisely what separates Schopenhauer decisively from one of the most significant personalities of recent times. While Schopenhauer's ideal is a man who has overcome everything that external life can give him by way of pleasure and pain, and waits only for the last traces holding his body together to be dissolved, Goethe sets before us in his Faust a striving character who passes from desire to satisfaction and from satisfaction to desire, until finally he has purified himself and transformed his desires to such a degree that the holiest element that can illuminate our life becomes his passion. He does not stand and wait until the last traces of his earthly existence are extinguished, but speaks the great words: "Not in aeons will the trace of my days on earth pass away."[63]

The sense and spirit of all this is presented by Goethe in his Faust just as in old age he described it to his secretary, Eckermann:[64] "For the rest you will admit, that the closing passage, when the redeemed soul is borne aloft, was very difficult to manage. With such supersensible, hardly imaginable things I could easily have lost myself in vagueness if I had not made use of clearly outlined figures and images from the Christian Church to give the requisite form and substance to my poetic intentions."

So it is that Faust climbs the ladder of existence, represented in Christian symbols, from mortal to immortal, from death to life.

We see in Schopenhauer the unmistakeable projection of Buddhist elements into our western way of thinking, so that his ideal man waits to reach the state of perfection until the last traces of his earth-existence have been erased, together with his body. And this vision, Schopenhauer believes, can interpret the figures created by Raphael and Correggio in their paintings. Goethe wished to set before us a man who strives towards a goal, well aware that whatever is achieved in earthly life must be enduring, interwoven with eternity. "Not in aeons will the trace of my days on earth pass away."

That is the true, realistic Christian impulse, which leads to the reawakening of our earthly deeds in a spiritualised form. That is the religion of resurrection. It is also a realistic philosophy in the true sense,

Metamorphoses of the Soul

for it knows how to draw down from spiritual heights the loftiest elements for our life in the world of the senses. Thus we can see in Goethe, like a dawning glow, the Christianity of the future, which has learnt to understand itself. This Christianity will recognise all the greatness and significance of Buddhism, but, by contrast with the Buddhist turning away from incarnations, it will recognise the value of each existence from one incarnation to the next. Thus Goethe, in a truly modern Christian sense, looks at a past which brought us to birth out of a world, and at present in which whatever we achieve—if only its fruits are rightly grasped—can never pass away. When, therefore, he links man to the universal in the true spiritual-scientific sense, he cannot but join him on the other side to the true content of Christianity. Thus in his *Urworte-Orphisch* he says:

> As on the day that lent thee earthly being,
> The Sun took salutation from the planets,
> So didst thou start thy course and so hast sped it,
> According to the law of thy first sending.
> So must thou be: thyself thou canst not flee from.
> Thus have the Sibyls, thus the prophets, spoken.

Goethe could not write in this way, describing the connection of man with the whole world, without indicating that the human being, born out of the constellations of existence, is in the world as something that can never pass away but must celebrate its resurrection in spiritualised form. Hence to these lines he added two more:

> No time, no power, can bring to dissolution
> The form once cast in living evolution.

And we can say: No time and no power can destroy what is achieved in time and ripens as fruit for eternity.

LECTURE 9
Something about the Moon in the Light of Spiritual Science

Berlin, 9th December, 1909

The lecture I am to give today puts me in a difficult position. I want to make some remarks which fall outside the way of thinking now called "scientific". Since the views of most people are largely formed by the ideas generally current in scientific and popular-scientific circles, and since the subject-matter of this lecture will be far removed from any such ideas, the public at large may be inclined to regard my statements as mere fancies, derived from quite arbitrary cogitations, rather than for what they really are: the outcome of spiritual-scientific research.

I would ask you, therefore, to take this lecture as a sort of episode in our winter series, intended to point in a direction to which I am not likely to return this year, though it may occupy us further next year. The reason for touching on it now, is to show that what we are dealing with this winter as a science of the soul, branches out in many ways that lead from the immediate realm of human soul-life to the great connections we find in the wide universe, the whole cosmos.

Finally, I must ask you to remember that this lecture will deal only with one short chapter from a very large volume. It must be seen in strict relation to its title, *"Something about the Moon in the Light of Spiritual Science"*. It will not attempt to be in any way exhaustive.

In all sorts of popular books you will find this or that said about the moon from the standpoint of science today. But all you can learn from these sources or from the scientific literature will leave you quite unsatisfied as regards the real questions concerning this strange companion of the earth. As the 19th century advanced, the statements of science with regard to the moon became more and more cautious, but also less frequent; but today they will occupy us hardly at all. The picture of the moon's surface given by telescopes and astronomical photography, the descriptions of its surface-markings as crater-like formations, grooves,

Metamorphoses of the Soul

plains and valleys and suchlike, and the consequent impressions one can gain of the purely spatial countenance of the moon—all this will not concern us. The question for us today is a truly spiritual-scientific one— whether the moon has any special influence on or significance for human life on earth.

A significance of this kind has been spoken of from various points of view in the course of past centuries. And since everything that happens on earth, year in and year out, is related to the changing position of the earth relative to the sun, and is subject to the vast influence of the sun's light and heat, it was natural to wonder whether that other heavenly luminary, the moon, might not have some importance for life on earth, and especially for human life.

In the comparatively recent past, people were inclined to speak of the moon as having a fairly powerful influence on earthly life. Quite apart from the fact that it has long been customary to attribute to the moon's attraction the so-called ebb and flow of the sea, the moon has always been regarded as affecting weather conditions on earth. Moreover, as late as the first half of the 19th century, serious scientists and doctors collated observations of how the moon in its various phases had a definite effect on certain illnesses, and even on the course of human life as a whole. It was then by no means a mere popular superstition to consider the influence of the moon in relation to the ups and downs of fever, of asthma, of goitre and the like; there were still doctors who recorded such cases because they felt compelled to believe that the phases of the moon had some influence on the course of human life and on health and disease in particular.

With the rise of that scientific way of thinking which had its dawn and sunrise in the middle of the 19th century, the inclination to allow the moon any influence on human life diminished continuously. Only the belief that the moon causes the tides of the sea survived. And there was one very important scientist, Schleiden,[65] who poured out the vials of his wrath on those who still believed in the influence of the moon, even if it were only on the weather or on some other terrestrial phenomena. Schleiden, who had done outstanding work in his own sphere by his discovery of the significance of the plant-cell, launched a vehement attack on another German natural scientist, Gustav Theodor Fechner,[66] notable especially for directing attention to certain subtle or frontier aspects of research. Thus in his *Zend Avesta* Fechner tried to show that the life of plants is endowed with soul, while in his *Introduction to Aesthetics* and his *Elements of Psychophysics* he achieved a great deal for the more intimate aspects of natural science. It may be better not to discuss this celebrated controversy about the moon without saying

Something about the Moon

a little more about Fechner himself.

Fechner was an investigator who tried, with immense assiduity and great care and precision, to bring together the external facts in various fields of research; but he also used a method of analogies in order to show, for example, that all the phenomena of plant-life, and not only of human life, are ensouled. Starting with the phenomena of human life as it runs its course, he took similar facts and phenomena as they appear to observation in, let us say, the life of the earth, or of a whole solar system, or of the plant-world. When he compared these phenomena with those of human life, he found one analogy after another. Hence he concluded—to put it roughly—that in studying human life, with its ensoulment, we observe the occurence of certain phenomena; and if in observing other phenomena we can establish certain similarities with human life, why should we not recognise the other phenomena as being also "ensouled"?

Anyone who stands on the ground of Spiritual Science, and is used to examining everything related to the spiritual in as strictly scientific a sense as the natural scientist applies to his studies of external phenomena, will feel that a good deal of what Fechner works out so cleverly is merely an ingenious game; and however stimulating a game of this kind may be, the greatest care must be taken in dealing with mere analogies. When a stimulating thinker such as Fechner employs this method, his work may be very interesting. But there are people of whom it can justly be said that they would like to solve the riddles of the world with as little knowledge and as much comfort as possible. And if they lean on Fechner and make his methods their own, we must remember that an imitator or a copyist does not by any means call forth in us the same feelings of satisfaction as does the man who was first in his own field—a man who we recognise as gifted and stimulating, even though we cannot credit him with anything more.

We have no need to characterise Schleiden any further than by saying that he discovered the significance of the plant-cell. Clearly such a man, who directed all his perceptive and cognitive faculties towards the immediately real—that is, towards what can be perceived with external instruments—will have little sympathy for analogies or with anything else that Fechner spoke of in his endeavours to show that plants are ensouled; for in Schleiden's view they are made up of single cells, and this fact naturally seemed to him, as its discoverer, a wonderful thing. So for Schleiden it was something of an outrage that speculations, with this brilliant model available as a starting-point, should prefer to deal with some even subtler relationships in nature. It was particularly Fechner's method of analogies that aroused Schleiden's wrath, and in this connection he touched on the question of the moon. With reference not only to Fechner but to all those who clung to the centuries-old tradition of attributing to the moon all sorts of influences on the weather, etc., he said that for these people the moon was like a cat in the house, held responsible for everything that cannot be otherwise explained.

Fechner naturally felt challenged as he was the main target of these attacks. He at once embarked on a work which—whether or not we agree with it—is highly stimulating. Although many details in it have since been corrected, Fechner's pamphlet, "Schleiden and the Moon", published in 1856, is remarkably interesting. He had no need to go into the influence of the moon on the ebb and flow of the tides, for this was admitted even by Schleiden. It was the supposed connection of the moon with weather conditions that made the moon, for him, the cat of scientific research. Fechner therefore set out to investigate the very facts that his opponent brought against him, and from this material he drew some notable conclusions. Anyone who cares to check his procedure will find that in this investigation Fechner was an exceptionally cautious worker with a thoroughly scientific approach. His first conclusion from a mass of facts—which I need not repeat, for anyone can read them for himself—was that the quantity and frequency of rainfall were in many cases shown to be greater with a waxing than with a waning moon: greater when the moon approached the earth, smaller when it receded; and the proportion of rainfall during a waxing moon to that during the wane was 107:100. The recorded observations he used did not cover a few years only; some of them extended over many decades and concerned not a single locality but many parts of Europe.

In order to exclude chance effects, Fechner now assumed that some other condition, excluding the moon, might have produced this proportion of 107:100. He then studied weather conditions on the odd and even dates of the moon's phases, for he said that if the waning and waxing were not the cause, the odd and even days of the month would produce similar results. But that was not the case. Quite different figures emerged: the relationship was not constant but variable, so that here it could be attributed to chance.

Fechner himself realised that he had not achieved any world-shattering result; he had to recognise that the moon had no very great influence on the weather, but the facts did point to some influence. And he had, as you will have seen, proceeded quite scientifically, taking account only of observations carefully recorded for definite places. He made similar researches in relation to fevers and other bodily phenomena, and

Something about the Moon

here too he obtained small positive results. It could hardly be denied that phenomena of this kind may take a different course under the waxing and under the waning moon. Thus the old view of the moon fought its last fight in the middle of the 19th century through the work of this highly gifted man, Fechner.

This example shows very well how wrong it is to accept the increasingly common assertion that science compels us to talk no more about the spiritual background of things, for science—we are assured—is on the verge of learning how to combine simple materials in such a way as to produce living substance. It is agreed that we have far to go before we can make protein from its constituents—carbon, hydrogen, oxygen and so on—but the whole tendency of science is to make us admit that one day it will be done. When it has been done, the only tenable outlook—so we are told by those who make these assertions—will be a monistic one which holds that a living, thinking being is made up of nothing but an assembly of material elements.

Anyone who talks in this vein will have drawn on the latest aims and achievements of science to convince himself that we are not justified in postulating something spiritual behind what we perceive with our senses or are told by external science; for happily—he will feel—we are long past the days when it could be claimed that some kind of vague life-wisdom lies behind the sense-perceptible world.

At this point we may well ask. Is it really science that compels us to reject spiritual research? Is that a scientific conclusion? I want to remain entirely on the ground of those who believe that in the not too distant future it will be possible to produce living protein out of simple substances. Is there anything in that which compels us to say that life is materially constituted and that we must not look anywhere for the spirit?

An ordinary historical observation will show how unnecessary this conclusion is. There was a time when it was believed not only that carbon, hydrogen, etc., could be used to produce living protein, but that a whole man could be built up from the necessary ingredients in a retort. The worth of this belief need not concern us—you can read a poetical treatment of it in the second part of *Faust*. The point is that there were times when people really believed—however crazy it may seem to us—that Homunculus could be put together out of separate components. Yet in those times no-one doubted that behind the sense-perceptible was the spirit. Hence you can prove historically that no "science" can compel us to reject the spirit, for this depends on something quite different—on whether or not a capacity to discern the spirit is there. Neither the science of today nor the science of tomorrow can ever compel us to reject the spirit. We can take a perfectly scientific standpoint, but whether or not we reject the spirit does not depend on science. It depends on whether or not we are able to discern the spirit, and science cannot determine that.

So, without agreeing from the spiritual-scientific point of view either with Schleiden or with Fechner, we can understand that Schleiden, with his eyes fixed on the sense-world, rejected everything that might be sought as soul or spirit behind the phenomena. But it was not on scientific grounds that he took this attitude; he was simply so inured to looking at visible things that he had no sympathy for anything else. Fechner was a quite different sort of man; his outlook embraced the spiritual, and though he made one error after another he was a man of different quality, one who sought the spirit. Hence his tendency was not to reject but to clarify the significance of the subtler influences of the heavenly bodies on one another. He said to himself: When I look at the moon, it is not for me merely the slagheap it looks like through a telescope; it is ensouled, as are all other bodies. Hence the moon-soul must have effects on the earth-soul, and these come to expression below the surface of ordinary life or in weather phenomena.

Now it is noteworthy, and has often been pointed out here, that the method of spiritual-scientific research is directed towards the practical, and that the best proofs of what it has to say can be found in everyday life. And that is just how Fechner set about defending his views. He suggested that the dispute between Schleiden and himself over the moon could perhaps be best settled by their wives. He said: "We both need rainwater for washing, and it could be collected in relation to weather conditions. Since Schleiden and I live under the same roof and can collect water at definite times, I suggest that my wife collects it during the waxing moon and Schleiden's wife during the wane. I am sure she will agree in order not to put her husband's theory to shame, the more so as she sets no great store by it. The result will be that my wife will have an extra can for every fourteen cans collected by Frau Schleiden, but for the sake of overcoming a preconceived opinion she will surely make this sacrifice."[67]

Here, then, we have drawn on the history of thought to show how the moon and its influence on the earth were regarded not very long ago. Nowadays one might say that people are more advanced in their scientific outlook—as they would call it—and so have gone a step beyond Schleiden in the sense that they would treat as a superstitious dreamer anyone who clung to the belief that the moon could have anything to do with weather conditions and the like. Even among quite sensible people today you will find no other opinion than that the

Something about the Moon

moon has influence only on the tides; all other opinions having been superseded.

If we take the standpoint of Spiritual Science, we are of course not obliged to swear to everything that was once part of popular belief. That would be to confuse Spiritual Science with superstition. Quite often today we encounter a piece of superstition—which is really a misunderstood popular belief and are told it is part of Spiritual Science. A superstition about the moon can indeed be seen at every streetcorner, for it is well known that an emblem of the moon is attached to our barbers' shops—why? Because it was once generally believed that the sharpness of a razor was connected with a waxing moon. In fact there were times when no-one would have cared to shear a sheep during the wane, for he would have believed that the wool would then not grow again. This is a superstition very easy to disprove, for anyone who shaves knows that the beard grows again during the wane. In this realm it is just as easy to mock as it is hard, on the other side, to see clearly. For we are coming now to a particular question where at last we touch on Spiritual Science. It concerns the ebb and flow of the tides, universally regarded as coming under the influence of the moon.

The flood-tide is thought to be obviously connected with the attractive force of the moon, and is looked for when the moon reaches its meridian. When the moon leaves the meridian, the flood is expected to change to ebb. But we need only remark that in many places ebb and flow occur twice, while the moon stands at the meridian only once during the same period. And there are other facts. You can learn from travel-books that in many parts of the earth the flood by no means coincides with the moon's meridian; in some places it occurs up to two and a half hours later. Certainly, science has thought up excuses to account for this: we are told that the flood is retarded. But there are also certain springs which show an indubitable ebb and flow; in some cases the well ebbs when the ocean tide is at flood, and *vice versa*. We are told that these cases, too, are examples of retarded ebb or flow— in some cases so retarded as to run into the other phase. Of course this kind of explanation can explain almost anything.

One question has been rightly asked: whence does the moon get this power to attract the sea? The moon is much smaller than the earth and has only about a seventieth of the earth's attractive power, while to set the great masses of the sea into motion would require millions of horse-power. Julius Robert Mayer[68] made some interesting calculations on this question and it leads on to numerous other problems. Hence we can say: Here is something which is regarded as scientifically irrefutable, and yet, although no objections to it are heard, it is in fact highly vulnerable.

One very significant fact, however, remains. Although the position and influence of the moon are such that it is hard to speak of an immediate relation of cause and effect, it holds true that a definite flood occurs every day—in relation to the moon's meridian—about fifty minutes later than on the previous day. The regular sequence of ebb and flow does therefore *correspond* to the course of the moon, and that is the most significant fact of all. Thus we cannot speak of the moon at its meridian as having an actual influence on flow and ebb, but we can say that the course of the moon's orbit does stand in a certain correspondence with the course of the tides.

Now, to go a little way into the spiritual-scientific way of thinking, I would like to refer to a similar fact which gave Goethe a great deal of trouble. Most people know very little about the preoccupations of this great genius of modern times, but anyone who, like myself, has spent many years in the study of Goethe's scientific writings and has seen his manuscripts in the Goethe-Schiller Archives at Weimar, makes some surprising discoveries. He will, for example, come upon the preliminary notes which Goethe later condensed into a few pages as his meteorology.[69] He pursued these inquiries with enormous diligence and assiduity. Again and again he got his friends to collect facts and figures for him to tabulate. The purpose of these extensive studies was to show that the level of barometric pressure at various places is not due to chance but varies in some quite regular way. And Goethe did in fact assemble a great deal of evidence which indicated that in all sorts of places the rise and fall of the barometer were subject to a law which extended all round the globe. He hoped to disprove the assumption that air pressure depends entirely on external influences. He knew, of course, that densification and rarefaction of the air, resulting in pressure changes, were generally attributed to the moon, sun and other cosmic factors. He wanted to prove that whatever the positions of the constellations, whatever the effects of sun and moon on the atmosphere, a constant regularity in the rise and fall of air pressure prevails all round the globe. Hence he wished to show that in the earth itself lay the causes of the rise and fall of the barometer, for he believed that the earth is not the dead body it is usually taken to be, but is permeated by invisible elements from which all life flows, just as man has, in addition to his physical body, invisible elements which permeate him. And just as man has his in-breathing and out-breathing, where he draws in or releases air, so does the earth, as a living being, breathe in and out. And this in-breathing and out-breathing of the earth, as manifestations of its inner life, are registered externally in the rise and fall of the mercury in

Something about the Moon

the barometer. Thus we have in Goethe a man who was convinced that the earth is a being imbued with soul and which behaves in ways that are comparable to the breathing process in human beings. Moreover, Goethe once said to Eckermann that he regarded the ebb and flow of the tides as a further expression of the inner vitality, the life-process, of the earth.[70]

Goethe was by no means the only great thinker who looked with a spiritual eye on such things from this point of view. Materialistically minded people will of course find all this laughable; but among men who have a feeling for life, be it on such a particular level or more in general, there will always be those with ideas similar to Goethe's— for example, Leonardo da Vinci. In his outstanding book, where he sets out his comprehensive scientific views, the height of achievement for those times, we find him saying—and not meaning it merely as an analogy—that he really regarded the solid rocks as the skeleton of the earth, and that the rivers, streams and watercourses can truly be compared to the blood circulation in man.[71] There you will find it stated also that ebb and flow are connected with a regular rhythm in the inner life of the earth. Kepler, too, spoke in a similar vein when he said that the earth could be regarded in certain respects as a gigantic whale and that ebb and flow were the in-breathing and out-breathing of this huge creature.[72]

Let us now compare the facts mentioned earlier with such views as Goethe's on ebb and flow. Let us use the findings of Spiritual Science and our previous conclusions about the phases of the moon and the tides in relation, for example, to Goethe's views on the earth's inner life and breathing. For this we must build on the conclusions of Spiritual Science, which can be established only if researches are pursued by spiritual-scientific methods. Here we enter the highly dangerous realm where those who believe they have a firm foothold in modern science will talk about the fantasies of Spiritual Science. Well, let them talk. It would be better if they were to take what is given as a stimulus; then they would be able to find proofs through a more intimate consideration of life.

In order to approach in the right way what the spiritual scientist has to say, let us consider man himself in relation to the world around him. As far as Spiritual Science is concerned, man has his origins not in the sense-world, but also in the spiritual foundations which lie behind the external physical world. Thus it is only as a being of the senses that man is born from out of the sense-world. In so far as he is permeated with soul and spirit, he is born from out of the soul and spirit of the cosmos. And it is only when we find the way from man's soul and spirit to the soul and spirit of the cosmos that we are enabled to see something of the connection between the two.

In previous lectures we have discussed various phenomena of the inner soul-life of man. We found the soul to be not merely the nebulous something that it is for modern psychology. Among its members we distinguished, first, what we called the Sentient Soul. In this soul the ego, though dimly and scarcely aware of itself, experiences the impulses of pleasure and pain and everything that comes to it from the outer world through the sentient body. The ego is present within the life of the Sentient Soul, but as yet knows nothing of itself. Then the ego develops further and the soul advances to the stage of the Intellectual Soul or Mind Soul. And when the ego has carried still further its work on the soul, the Intellectual Soul gives rise to the Consciousness Soul. Thus in the structure of the human soul we distinguish three members: Sentient Soul, Intellectual Soul and Consciousness Soul.

The ego continues to work on these three members and brings man nearer and nearer to the peak of his developments. But these three members, since they carry out their work through man, have to live in his corporeal structure; in that way only can they accomplish their tasks. The Sentient Soul uses as its instrument the sentient body; the Intellectual Soul uses the etheric body. The Consciousness Soul is the first to use the physical body as bearer and instrument. Thus in man's corporeal structure we have first the physical body, which he has in common with the minerals. Next we have in man a higher part which he has in common with the plant world and everything that lives. The functions of growth, nutrition and reproduction in the plant are active also in man, but in man they are connected with the Intellectual Soul. The plant's etheric body is not permeated by the Intellectual Soul, as is the etheric body in man, just as the physical body is permeated by the Consciousness Soul. That which forms crystals in the mineral realm is permeated in man by the Consciousness Soul. In animals the astral body is the bearer of impulses and emotions; in man the astral body is inwardly deepened and is the bearer of the Sentient Soul. Thus the human soul, made up of Sentient Soul, Intellectual Soul and Consciousness Soul, dwells in his threefold corporeality, in the sentient body, etheric body and physical body respectively.

That is man's condition while he is awake. During sleep it is different. Then, leaving his physical and etheric bodies behind in bed, he goes out from them with his ego and astral body, together with those parts of his soul which permeate his etheric and physical bodies as Intellectual Soul and Consciousness Soul. Thus during sleep he lives in a spiritual world which he cannot perceive, simply because here on earth he is

Something about the Moon

obliged to use his physical and etheric bodies as instruments for perceiving the surrounding world. When in sleep he lays these instruments aside, he is unable to perceive the spiritual world, since in ordinary life today he lacks the organs for it.

Now there is something else to say about these states of waking and sleeping. Our waking life is directly connected with the course of the sun—though indeed this is no longer quite true of people today, especially in towns. But if we look at simple country life, where this relation between outer nature and human living still largely prevails, we find that for most of the time people are awake while the sun is up and asleep while the sun is down. This regular alternation of waking and sleeping corresponds to the regular action of sunlight on the earth and all that springs from it. And it is not merely a picturesque way of speaking but deeply true to say that in the morning the sun recalls into the physical body the astral body and ego, together with the Sentient Soul, the Intellectual Soul and the Consciousness Soul; and while he is awake man sees everything around him by means of the sun and its radiance. And when man has once more united all the members of his being in daylight consciousness, it is the sun which summons him to ordinary life. We shall now easily recognise, if we are not taking a superficial view of these things, *how* the sun regulates the relationship of man to itself and to the earth. Let us now look more closely at three aspects of this relationship.

With regard to his threefold soul-nature, comprising Sentient Soul, Intellectual Soul and Consciousness Soul, man is inwardly independent; but he is not with regard to their bearers, the astral, etheric and physical bodies. These three sheaths are built up from the outer universe, and in order that they may serve man in his waking life, they are built up through the relationship between sun and earth.

As we have seen, the Sentient Soul lives in its instrument, the sentient body. The sentient body owes its characteristics to the region which a man calls his home. Everyone has a home somewhere, and it matters whether he is born in Europe or America or Australia. For the physical and etheric bodies it makes no direct difference, but it does matter directly for the sentient body. Although man is gradually becoming more free from these effects on his sentient body, we still have to say: human beings whose roots are in their native soil, human beings in whom a feeling for their homeland is particularly strong, who have not yet overcome by strength of soul the power of the physical and are drawn to their place of birth—if such human beings have to move to another region, they are not only apt to become bad-tempered and morose, but may actually fall ill. Sometimes, then, the mere prospect of returning home is enough to restore them to health, for the source of their illness is not in the physical body or in the etheric body but in their sentient body, whose moods, emotions and desires spring directly from the environment of their native land.

Through higher development, which enhances his freedom, man will overcome the influences which bind him to his native soil; but a comprehensive view shows that a man's situation on earth varies in accordance with the relation of the place where he lives to the sun; for the angle at which the sun's rays strike the earth varies from place to place. We can indeed trace in certain instinctive activities, which then become culturally assimilated, that they derive partially from the homeland of the people concerned.

Let us take two examples: the use of iron and the milking of animals for food. We shall find that it is only in certain areas of Europe, Asia and Africa that these two practices developed. In other areas they were unknown in early times. And where they came into use later on, they were introduced by emigrants from Europe. We can trace exactly how throughout Siberia the milking of animals dates from remote antiquity, and extends only as far as the Behring Sea; there is no record of it among the original inhabitants of America. It is similar with iron.

Thus we can see how certain instincts which exist in the sentient body are connected with a particular region where people live, and how they are therefore dependent in the first place on the relation of sun to earth.

A second dependence concerns the etheric body. As the bearer of the Intellectual Soul, the etheric body shows itself to be dependent in its activity on the seasons of the year; hence on the relation of sun to earth expressed in the course of the seasons. A direct proof of this can of course come only through Spiritual Science, but you can convince yourselves by external facts that this statement is correct. For example, it is only in regions where a balanced alternation of seasons occurs that the inner activity of the soul as Intellectual Soul can develop; this means that only in such regions can a necessary bearer or instrument of the Intellectual Soul evolve in the etheric body of man. In the far north we find that when elements of culture are brought in from elsewhere, the soul has great difficulty in struggling with the etheric body, which is having to live under conditions characterised by excessively long winters and short summers. The Intellectual Soul will then find it impossible to forge out of the etheric body an instrument it can easily handle.

If we go to the tropics, we find that the lack of regular seasons

Something about the Moon

produces a kind of apathy. Just as the forces of plant life vary in the course of the year, so do the forces in man's etheric body: they find expression in the joy of spring, the longing for summer, the melancholy of autumn, the desolation of winter. These regular changes are necessary if a proper instrument for the Intellectual Soul is to be created in the human etheric body. Thus we see again how the sun affects human beings through its changing relation to the earth.

Now let us take the physical body. If the Consciousness Soul is to work right into the physical body, we must follow in ordinary life a rhythm similar to the alternation of day and night. Anyone who never slept would soon notice that he was unable to control effectively his thoughts about the world around him. A regular alternation of waking and sleeping builds up our physical body in a way that can provide an instrument for the Consciousness Soul. Thus we have now seen how man's three bodies, astral, etheric and physical, are built up by the sun.

But what external influences play into the human being while he is asleep, while he is living in the spiritual world and has left his physical and etheric bodies behind?

While we are asleep we get something from the spiritual world to replace the forces that have been used up by our activities during the preceding day. Is it possible in this case also to point to an external influence, as we did with regard to the daytime waking hours? Yes, it is, and what we find is in remarkable accord with the length of the phases of the moon. I am not maintaining that this external influence coincides exactly with the moon's phases, or that the phases themelves produce corresponding effects, but only that the course of these effects is comparable with the course of the phases of the moon. I will give two examples to show what I mean.

You will be well aware that people who are given to creative thoughts and the free play of imagination are not equally productive at all times. Poets, for example, if they are honest with themselves, have to admit now and then that they are out of tune, unable to write anything. People who observe this in themselves know that the productive periods, for which a certain imaginative frame of mind and a warmth of feeling are necessary, alternate in a remarkable way with periods when nothing can be accomplished. They know, too, that the soul has a fourteen-day period of productivity, after which anyone who has to do with creative thinking goes through an empty period, when the soul is like a squeezed out lemon. During this empty period, however, he can apply himself to working over what he has done. If artists and authors would take note of this, they would soon see how true it is.

This alternation of periods is influenced not by daytime conditions, but by the times when the soul and the ego are outside the physical and etheric bodies. And so, for a fourteen-day period, productive forces are, as it were, poured into the human being while he is independent of his physical and etheric bodies, and then, during the next fourteen days, no such forces are poured in. That is the rhythm. It applies to all human beings, but is more clearly evident in the sort of people we have just mentioned.

Much clearer still is the evidence from genuine spiritual research. This is not the kind of research that can be undertaken whenever one chooses, but it is dependant on a rhythmical pattern. This point has hardly ever been mentioned anywhere, but it is so. During spiritual research one is not sleeping—the world-spirit does not bestow its gifts in sleep! The physical body is inactive with regard to the outer world, yet one is not asleep, although the physical and etheric bodies have been left behind. Meditation, concentration and so on have strengthened the researcher's faculties to such a degree that consciousness is not blotted out when it goes forth from the physical body. Sleep does not supervene and the spiritual world can be perceived. For the modern spiritual researcher there are two periods: one of fourteen days when he can make observations: he feels particularly strong and communications from the spiritual world press in on him from all sides. Then comes a period during which he is particularly well able, thanks to the forces just received, to penetrate with his thinking the illuminations, the imaginations and inspirations that have come to him from the spiritual world, to work over them so that they may acquire a strictly scientific form. Inspiration and the technique of thinking follow a rhythmical course. The spiritual researcher does not need to bring about a co-ordination with external facts; he simply sees how these periods occur in alternation, as do full moon and new moon, with their intervening quarters. But it is only their rhythmical course that has a parallel in the alternation of full and new moon. The period of inspiration does not coincide with full moon or the working over period with new moon. All we can say is that a comparison is possible between the two periods and full and new moon. Why should this be so?

When we study our earth, we find that it has evolved out of an earlier state. Just as each one of us has come in soul and spirit from a former incarnation, so has the earth emerged from a former planetary incarnation. But our earth retains relics of events which occurred under earlier conditions during its previous incarnation. And these relics are to be found in the course of the moon round the earth, as we see it today. From a spiritual-scientific point of view the moon is reckoned as

Something about the Moon

part of the earth. For what is it that keeps the moon circling round the earth? It is the earth itself, and here spiritual science and external science are in complete agreement. External science, too, regards the moon as having been split off from the earth, and having gained the force which keeps it in orbit through having once formed part of the earth. Thus the orbiting moon represents simply an earlier condition of the earth. The earth itself has retained in its satellite these earlier conditions because it needs to have them shining into the present. Can we find any reason for this need?

Let us take man himself and observe how he lives as a soul in his body and how he is exposed to the course of the sun. We then must say: For normal consciousness today, everything associated with the sun is restricted to the life between birth and death. This is something you can test—ask yourselves whether what normal consciousness experiences during waking hours, in its threefold dependence on native place, the changing seasons and the alternation of day and night, is not restricted to the life between birth and death. Man would have nothing else in his consciousness, nothing more would illuminate it, if there were only this action of the sun on the earth and only this relation between earth and sun. That which plays over from one incarnation to the next and appears again in a new life, must be sought in the soul-spiritual element which permeates man's outer body and during sleep passes as astral body and ego out of the physical and etheric bodies. At death also it leaves the body, and reappears in a new form at the next incarnation. Here there is a rhythm which directs our attention to a similar rhythm associated with the moon.

If now we consider human evolution, we see that the work of the ego on the Sentient Soul, Intellectual Soul and Consciousness Soul has developed only on earth under the conditions that prevail between earth and sun. But the earth's relation to the moon reflects a former condition in its own evolution. Man's present phase of evolution, through Sentient Soul, Intellectual Soul and Consciousness Soul, points to a period during which the bearers of the above soul-members, the astral, etheric and physical bodies, were being prepared. Then, just as the action of the sun is now still necessary for the proper development of these three bearers, the moon forces were at work in preparing them. Today the moon forces were once in harmony with man and prepared him to be what he is today; likewise the earth during its moon condition prepared our present earth. Thus we can say that the lower nature of man, on which are built the Sentient Soul, Intellectual Soul and Consciousness Soul, points back to earlier conditions which the earth has preserved in the orbit of the moon as we see it today.

We can see, too, how man's inner being, as he passes from one incarnation to the next, must have a rhythm corresponding to the moon's. During earlier stages of the earth's evolution, it was not the transitory physical that was associated with the moon, but the inner activity which was working on this physical, just as the external physical is today being worked on by the sun. The earth has preserved in the moon something of its earlier conditions, and so has man in his inner, eternal being. In this inner being he is now evolving those higher qualities which were formerly an external influence and which are now to be developed by his own inner capacities.

An essential point we must emphasise is that man grows out of these external influences. He becomes more independent all the time— e.g., he can sleep by day and stay awake at night. But he still has to order his waking and sleeping in accordance with the rhythm of the sun; he has to maintain the rhythm within himself. In earlier times, inner day and night corresponded closely to the sun's day and night; man was then more closely bound to his native soil. He becomes free and independent precisely by inwardly liberating the rhythm under which he lives; by retaining it as a rhythm, but no longer dependent on the outer world. It is as if we had a clock marked for 24 hours but set in such a way that it does not correspond with external time; e.g., when the clock says it is 12 o'clock, it is not 12 o'clock by the sun. Thus although the clock follows a 24-hour rhythm, the time it shows is its own, not that of the sun.

Thus man frees himself inwardly by making the external rhythm into an inner one. He has long since freed himself from the rhythm which connected his inner being with the moon. Hence we have emphasised that man lives through the phases of the moon inwardly, but these experiences are not caused by the moon in the sky. The course of the moon shows a similar rhythm because man has retained the rhythm inwardly, though outwardly he has made himself free and independent of it.

We are led in this way to regard the earth as a living being, but since it shows us only its physical body, with no evident signs of life or feeling or knowledge, its condition is nearer to that of the moon. Now we can understand why it is wrong, even taking only the external facts, to speak of a direct influence of the moon on the tides, and why we can say only that the ebb and flow of the tides corresponds to the phases of the moon. The tides, as well as the course of the moon are caused by deeper spiritual forces in the living earth.

Thus we see how Spiritual Science helps us to clarify external facts

Something about the Moon

in a wonderful way. The tides correspond to an inner process in the living earth, which produces them and also the orbit of the moon.[73] If you take the findings of Spiritual Science and then go through all the books where the phases of moon and earth and tides are recorded, you will understand the true relations between moon and earth and moon and man.

You can easily see that if a man loses his independence and sinks from a fully conscious into a less conscious or unconscious condition, he will regress to earlier stages of evolution. Man advanced from unconsciousness to his present state of consciousness, from his earlier dependence on the moon and its influence to his present independence from the moon and his dependence on the sun.

Because man was once directly dependent on the moon, it follows that if his consciousness is damped down, its functioning will be ordered by the course of the moon. This is an atavistic effect which brings out man's old connection with the moon's phases. A characteristic of mediums is that their consciousness is so far lowered that they revert to an earlier stage of evolution, and the old influence of the moon makes itself felt in them. It is similar in certain cases of illness where the consciousness is lowered. If you bear in mind the principles of Spiritual Science, you will be well able to understand these phenomena. The evidence for what Spiritual Science has to say can be found in all aspects of life.

One thing more. When someone is to be born again on earth after his sojourn in the spiritual world between death and a new birth, then, during the embryonic period, he passes through conditions which recall an earlier state of the earth. The embryonic period is still reckoned by science as covering ten lunar months; thus we have here a rhythm which runs its course through ten successive moon periods. We find also that each week in the ten-month period—that is, each phase of the moon—corresponds to a particular condition in the development of the embryo. Here, too, man has retained in himself the moon rhythm, as we may call it.

We could indeed mention a whole series of other phenomena connected with man's embryonic existence, before he emerges from the depths of nature into the light of day; they are of course not caused by the moon and do not coincide with the moon's phases but reflect the same rhythm, because they go back to primary causes which were present while the earth was passing through earlier conditions of existence.

Now I have thrown light on a subject which cannot be further illuminated in public. Thoughtful people will see that here a perspective is opened up into realms of life where Spiritual Science can indeed point the way to a great clarification of much in man that is hidden from external sunlight, that lies behind it. They are realms which have to be explored by a light different from the light of knowledge we have acquired through the light of the sun; namely by faculties which are not dependent on the service rendered by the sentient, etheric and physical bodies under the influence of the sun. A clairvoyant faculty makes itself independent of these three bodies; it can sink itself in inwardness and see into the spiritual world, and thus can open up a capacity for knowledge of what lies behind external sunlight and yet is full of light and clarity. But I must again emphasise that on the question of the moon an even more intimate light is needed if we are to get to the heart of it.

In conclusion, I am reminded of some verses by the German lyrical poet Wilhelm Müller: we are here concerned only with the last stanza. The moon is addressed and all sorts of intimate words pass between man and moon; and then, because the soul has spoken to the moon in a wonderful way:

> This little song, an evening round,
> A wanderer sings in full moonshine;
> Those who read it by candlelight
> Will always fail to get it right,
> Childishly simple though it is.[74]

That is rather how we should take what Spiritual Science has to say, as shown in our treatment of the moon and its significance for human life. The song of Spiritual Science about the moon can indeed be sung only if we have some understanding of the more intimate ideas of Spiritual Science. People who try to read the song by candlelight, by which I mean the telescope, and employ photographs of the moon, for so-called research—these people will hardly understand our song. But those who are ready to go even a little way into what life can tell us in all its aspects will say to themselves: It is really not so difficult! Anyone who seeks to understand the song that Spiritual Science sings about the moon—not by the candlelight of the telescope, but by the living light of the spirit, which shines even when all sense-impressions are absent— he will find that this song about the moon, and therefore about an important aspect of life, is truly quite easy, even if not childishly easy!

NOTES

1. The "Libellus de hominis convenienta" by Francis Joseph Philipp Count von Hoditz and Wolframitz is a manuscript which was discovered in the Fürstenberg Library in Prague and which was written approximately between 1696 and 1700.
2. Aristotle, 384-322 BC. Cf. the *Parva Naturalia*.
3. René Descartes, 1596-1650. Cf. for example the work "Meditationes de prima Philosophia", 1641/42.
4. With this answer Hoditz goes back to the Neo-Platonist Philo of Alexandria (see Rudolf Steiner's comments on him in *Christianity as a Mystical Fact*, Rudolf Steiner Press, London 1972) who in turn revives the Old Testament tradition; I Moses 1, 26/27.
5. Goethe: Winkelmann, "Antikes" and "Schönheit"; in: Goethe, *Werke*, Weimar Edition, vol.46 (Weimar, 1891).
6. Cf. for example Goethe's essay "Wenige Bemerkungen" in *Goethes Naturwissenschaftliche Schriften,* edited by Rudolf Steiner, Dornach, 1975, vol. I, p.107 or in "Entwurf einer Einleitung in die vergleichende Anatomie", *op. cit.,* p.262: "We learn to see with the eyes of the spirit, without which we grope around blindly as everywhere so also in natural science". Also *Faust* II, sc.1, 11.4667.
7. Immanuel Kant, 1724-1804. Cf. the chapter "The time of Kant and Goethe" in Rudolf Steiner's *The Riddles of Philosophy*, Anthroposophic Press, New York 1973.
8. Goethe, "Anschauende Urteilskraft" in: *Goethes Naturwissenschaftliche Schriften,* edited by Rudolf Steiner, Dornach, 1975, vol. I, p.115/116.
9. Cf. fundamental account of the stages of knowledge in Rudolf Steiner, *Occult Science, An Outline,* Rudolf Steiner Press, London 1979, in the chapter "Knowledge of the Higher Worlds".
10. The symbol of two intertwined triangles, the one pointing upwards, the other downwards.
11. Eliphas Levi, 1810-1875, occultist. Pseudonym for the originally catholic deacon Alphonse Louis Constant from Paris. *Dogme et Rituel de la haute Magie,* 2 vols, 1854 and 1856.
12. Philo of Alexandria (25 BC—50 AD) describes the life and thought of the Therapeutae in his work "De vital contemplativa". Cf. also Rudolf Steiner, *Christianity as Mystical Fact,* Rudolf Steiner Press, London 1972, p.137.
13. Decisive in this respect are the writings of Thomas Aquinas, especially the four books of the *Summa philosophica*. Cf. also Rudolf Steiner, *The Riddles of Philosophy* and *The Redemption of Thinking.*

Metamorphoses of the Soul

14. St. Augustine, 354—430 AD. Had the greatest influence of the Church Fathers on theology and philosophy.
15. *Faust* I, sc.1, 11.443-446.
16. Cf. Hermann Diels, *Die Fragmente der Vorsokratiker:* Herakleitos aus Ephesus, Nr. 45. Also: *The art and thought of Heraclitus.* An edition of the fragments with translation and commentary by Charles H. Kahn. CUP, Cambridge, 1979, No. XXXV.
18. Francesco Redi, 1626-98. Italian doctor, scientist and poet. Cf. his work *Osservazione intorno agli animali viventi che si trovano negli animali viventi,* 1684.
19. Giordano Bruno, born 1548, was burnt in 1600 in Rome as a heretic.
20. Arthur Schopenhauer, 1788-1860. Cf. his work *The World as Will and Representation,* Book I, par. 1.
21. Cf. for example the polemic "Eine Duplik" (1778), part I.
22. Edward Henry Harriman, 1848-1909. North American railway magnate.
23. Herman Grimm, 1828-1901, in his essay "Ernst Curtius, Heinrich von Treitschke, Leopold von Ranke", in: *Fragmente,* vol I, Berlin & Stuttgart, 1900, p.246.
24. Heinrich von Treitschke, 1834-96. German historian.
25. Karl Friedrich Solger, 1780-1819, from 1811 Professor of Philosophy in Berlin. Cf. *Erwin. Vier Gespräche über das Schöne und die Kunst,* 1815, and *Vorlesungen uber Asthetik,* ed. Heyse, 1829.
26. Robert Zimmermann, 1824-98. Professor in Vienna. Member of the school of Herbart. Cf. his *Asthetik,* 1858-65.
27. The first quotation is from the poem "Vermächtnis", 1829; the second is from the "Sprüche in Prosa" in vol V, p.402 of *Goethes Naturwissenschaftliche Schriften,* edited with a commentary by Rudolf Steiner, 5 vols, Dornach, 1975.
28. *Faust* I, 11.1224 and "Prometheus", a dramatic fragment, 1773.
29. From the poem "Sprichtwörtlich".
30. From the poem "Bei Betrachtung von Schillers Schädel", 1826.
31. *Faust* I, 11.1112-1117.
32. Cf. 19th Book, 1.137ff.
33. Johann Joachim Winkelmann, 1717-68. Cf. his "Geschichte der Kunst im Altertum", part II.
34. Agesander, a Rhodian sculptor, is mentioned by Pliny as the creator, together with Polydorus and Athenodorus, of the Laocoon

Notes

group, which dates from the period 42-21 BC. Now in the Vatican.

35. For his concept of asceticism see *The World as Will and Representation*, Book IV. Particularly from par. 68.

36. Cf. also the chapter "Sleep and Death" in Rudolf Steiner, *Occult Science, An Outline*.

37. Cf. also the chapter "Knowledge of the Higher Worlds" in Rudolf Steiner, *Occult Science, An Outline*.

38. Last verse of the poem "Selige Sehnsucht" from the *West-östliche Divan*.

39. See note 20.

40. Immanuel Kant, *Critique of Pure Reason*, Second Division, Book II, Chapter III, Section 4: "The impossibility of an Ontological Proof of the Existence of God".

41. Pythagoras of Samos, c. 580-495 BC. Cf. also Rudolf Steiner, *Christianity as Mystical Fact* and *The Riddles of Philosophy*.

42. From the poem "Das Höchste", 1795.

43. From the "Cherubinischen Wandersmann" by Angelus Silesius (1624-1677), Book I, Verse 289.

44. End of the poem "Welt und Ich" by Friedrich Rückert (1788-1866).

45. See note 5.

46. "Sprüche in Prosa", vol. V, p.495 of *Goethes Naturwissenschaftliche Schriften*, as note 27.

47. See "Entwurf einer Farbenlehre", vol. III, p.88 of *Goethes Naturwissenschaftliche Schriften*, as note 27.

48. Rudolf Steiner is here presumably refering to the sentence from Schopenhauer's introduction to his treatise "On Vision and Colours": ". . . That the colours which. . . appear to clothe the objects are really only in the eye".

49. In the conversation with Chancellor von Müller of 22nd January 1821.

50. "Sprüche in Prosa", vol. V, p.482 of *Goethes Naturwissenschaftliche Schriften*, as note 27.

51. In the conversation of 29th May 1814.

52. Johann Gottlieb Fichte, 1762—1814. "Vorbericht" to *Einige Vorlesungen über die Bestimmung des Gelehrten*.

53. Rudolf Steiner is here referring to the lectures on 22nd and 24th October 1908: "Goethe's Secret Revelation, Exoteric and Esoteric" and on 11th and 12th March 1909: "The Riddles in Goethe's Faust, Exoteric and Esoteric".

54. Cf. Pindar (522-c.448 BC) *Pythian Odes*, 8th Ode, 5th Epode.

Metamorphoses of the Soul

55. In connection with this lecture cf. also: Gautama Buddha's sayings from the middle Majjhimanikayo collection of the Pali Canon; *The Gospel of Buddha according to old Records* by Paul Carus, Chicago & London, 1917; Hermann Beckh, *Buddha and seine Lehre,* Stuttgart, 1958. For a contrast of Buddha and Christ also Rudolf Steiner in *Christianity as a Mystical Fact.*

56. Max Muller, 1823—1900, orientalist, religious and linguistic researcher. The quotation about the grunting pig attributed to him could not be traced.

57. Helena Petrovna Blavatsky, 1831—1891. She founded the Theosophical Society in New York together with H.S. Olcott in 1875, which soon thereafter transferred its headquarters to India.

58. Milindapanha (Milinda's Questions): Discussion between Menandros (Milinda), king of the Greco-Indian empire (c.110 BC), and the Buddhist saint Nagasena on the central questions of Buddhist dogma. Translated from the Pali by I.B. Horner, Luzac & Co., London, 1963/64.

59. Matth. 5, 3.
60. Matth. 3, 2.
61. Cf. Rudolf Steiner, *Riddles of Philosophy.*
62. See note 35.
63. *Faust* II, 11.11583/4.
64. Johann Peter Eckermann, *Conversations with Goethe in the Last Years of his Life,* conversation of 6th June 1831.
65. Matthias Jakob Schleiden, 1804-1881, Professor of Botany at the University of Jena.
66. Gustav Theodor Fechner, 1801-1887, Professor of Physics at the University of Leipzig. See *The Riddles of Philosophy,* 1973 edition, pp. 279, 375ff., 376, 380, 383. Published by Anthroposophic Press, New York.
67. G. Th. Fechner, *Professor Schleiden und der Mond,* Leipzig, 1856, p.156.
68. Julius Robert Mayer, 1814-1878, doctor and physicist, discovered the law of conservation of energy in 1842.
69. *Goethes Naturwissenschaftliche Schriften,* as note 27, vol. II, book 3, Meteorology, pp.323-398.
70. Johann Peter Eckermann, *Conversations with Goethe in the Last Years of his Life,* conversation of 11th April 1827.
71. See *Leonardo da Vinci, der Denker, Forscher und Poet,* from the published manuscripts; selection, translation and introduction by Marie Herzfeld (Jena, 1906), p.61 and following chapters.

Notes

72. Johannes Kepler, 1571-1630. Cf. for example in *Harmonices Mundi* book IV, chapter 7.

73. The correspondence between the moon's orbit and the tides can be led back to a joint cause, but the former does not cause the latter, just as the hand moving round the clock corresponds to the path of the sun, although no-one would suggest that the sun caused the clock-hand to move round.

74. Wilhelm Müller, 1794-1827, known for the cycles of poems "Die Winterreise" and "Die schöne Müllerin" which were set to music by Franz Schubert. This poem is the last verse from "Mondlied", from *Lieder der Griechen,* 2nd edition, Leipzig, 1844.

CONCERNING THE TRANSCRIPTS OF THE LECTURES

From Rudolf Steiner's autobiography *Mein Lebensgang* ("My Life"), Chapter 35, 1925. It was subsequently published in English, *Rudolf Steiner, An Autobiography*, 2nd Edition, Multimedia Pub. Corp., New York, 1980.

Two consequences of my anthroposophical activity are the books which were made accessible to the general public and an extensive series of lecture courses which were initially intended for private circulation and were available only to members of the Theosophical (later Anthroposophical) Society. The transcripts of the latter were taken down — some more accurately than others — during my lectures. But time did not permit me to undertake their correction. I, for my part, would have preferred spoken word to remain spoken word, but the members were in favour of private publication of the courses. And so it came about. If I had had time to correct the transcripts, the reservation "For Members Only" need not have been made from the very first. Now it has been dropped for over a year.

Here in "My Life" it is above all necessary to explain how the two — the publications in general and in private circulation — are accommodated in my elaboration of anthroposophy.

Whoever wishes to pursue my own inner conflict and toil in my effort to introduce anthroposophy to contemporary thought, must do so with the aid of the works in general circulation which include analysis of all forms of cognition of this age. Therein also lies that which crystallised within me in "spiritual vision" and from which came into existence the structure of anthroposophy, even if imperfect in many respects.

Apart from this obligation to construct anthroposophy and thereby to serve only that which ensues when communications from the spirit world are to be transmitted to modern civilisation, the need also arose to meet the claims which were manifested within the membership as a compulsion, a yearning of the soul.

Above all, many members were greatly disposed to hearing the gospels and the spiritual content of the Bible presented in an anthroposophical light. Courses were requested which were to examine such revelations to humanity.

Internal courses were held to meet this requirement. At these lectures only members were present who were initiated in anthroposophy. It was possible to speak to them as to those well-versed in anthroposophy. The delivery of these internal lectures was such as simply could not be communicated in written works intended for the general public.

In these closed circles I was able to discuss subjects which I would have had to present quite differently if they had been intended for a general public from the very first.

Thus in the duality of the public and private works there actually exists something of two-fold diverse origin. The wholly public writings are a result of that which struggled and toiled within me; in the private publications, the Society struggles and toils with me. I listen to the vibrations within the soul-life of the membership and within my own being, and the tone of the lectures arises from what I hear there.

Nowhere has even the slightest mention of anything been made which does not proceed from the substance of anthroposophy. No concessions can be made to any prejudices or presentiments existing within the membership. Whoever reads these private publications can accept them as a true representation of anthroposophical conviction. Thus when petitions became more urgent, the ruling as to the private circulation of these publications within the membership could be amended without any hesitation. Any errors occurring in transcripts which I have not been able to revise will however have to be tolerated.

The right to pass judgment on the content of any such private publication is nevertheless reserved to those possessing the prerequisite to do so. For the great majority of these publications, this is at least an anthroposophical knowledge of man and the universe, in so far as its essence is presented in anthroposophy, and of "the history of anthroposophy" such as it is derived from communications from the spirit world.

Complete Edition of the works of Rudolf Steiner in German, published by the Rudolf Steiner Verlag, Dornach, Switzerland, by whom all rights are reserved.

Writings

1. Works written between 1883 and 1925
2. Essays and articles written between 1882 and 1925
3. Letters, drafts, manuscripts, fragments, verses, inscriptions, meditative sayings, etc.

Lectures

1. Public Lectures
2. Lectures to Members of the Anthroposophical Society on general anthroposophical subjects.
   Lectures to Members on the history of the Anthroposophical Movement and Anthroposophical Society
3. Lectures and Courses on special branches of work:
   Art: Eurythmy, Speech and Drama, Music, Visual Arts,
   History of
   Art
   Education
   Medicine and Therapy
   Science
   Sociology and the Threefold Social Order
   Lectures given to Workmen at the Goetheanum

The total number of lectures amount to some six thousand, shorthand reports of which are available in the case of the great majority.

Reproductions and Sketches

Paintings in water colour, drawings, coloured diagrams, Eurythmy forms, etc.

When the Edition is complete the total number of volumes, each of a considerable size, will amount to several hundreds. A full and detailed Bibliographical Survey, with subjects, dates and places where the lectures were given is available. All the volumes can be obtained from the Rudolf Steiner Press in London as well as directly from the Rudolf Steiner Verlag, Dornach, Switzerland.